A Cornishman
Cruises to Venice

George Williams

ISBN-13: 978-1496130778

A Cornishman Cruises to Venice

CONTENTS

Introduction

With over twelve years of cruise holidays to look back on, there are several places that make me salivate with pleasure when I remember them. One of those places is the Italian city of Venice at the North Western end of the Adriatic Sea. Deb and I have been to Venice on numerous cruises, and on three different ships. Like several other special destinations, the arrival into the city and the farewell sail-away are all a part of the magical experience. Only a few of the passengers fail to be up by dawn to savour the arrival into one of the most amazing cities in the world.

Now here is a warning.

Venice is a city under threat from a rising sea level, and damage to the foundations of the city is being made worse by the sheer volume of ships and boats churning up the water of the canals.

This beautiful city has always suffered flooding from the very highest tides, but as the sea level has risen in recent years, these events are becoming worse, and more regular.

1

A massive project was initiated as far back as 2003 to address the flooding problem, and although many years late, it is hoped to be ready by 2018.

The 'MOSE' project involves building a series of 78 massive submergible flood gates at the Lido, Malamocco and Chioggia inlets to the Lagoon. At dangerously high tides, these flood gates will be raised to create a complete barrier between the Adriatic Sea and the Venetian Lagoon system.

Addressing the issue of damage caused by the canal water traffic is more difficult. The central area of the city does not have roads, and the only transport uses the canals. There are hundreds of boats going back and forth along the canals producing waves that create a constant storm in the water.

Venice relies on tourists, and many of those visitors arrive and leave on cruise ships. Although their numbers are small compared to the constant passage of water taxis, Vaporetti , and private boats, these cruise ships are a major threat to the canal side foundations.

The authorities of the city have projected that 2016 will see visits by over 500 cruise ships. They will bring around 1.55 million passengers to the city. These figures actually show a decline in ship and passenger numbers, but it is still an astounding number of people coming to Venice.

2

One factor causing the reduction in cruise ship numbers is that Venice is threatening to ban the larger ships, and to restrict the number of smaller vessels visiting the city.

Watching a cruise ship sailing serenely into the heart of the city suggests that these ships are travelling so slowly and so gently that surely they cannot be causing damage. But you only see what is above the water, and deep below the surface the ship is acting like a giant sink plunger stirring up the water.

Why are cruise ships a problem?

The answer to this question is all about their size.

When we talk about the size of a ship, it is usually in terms of its 'weight'. As an example the largest cruise ship in the world (2016) is the 'Harmony of the Seas' with an advertised weight just shy of 227,000 tonnes.

I would like to try and clear up the confusion about a ship's weight.

This 227,000 tonnes is not what a set of scales would show, if you could put the ship on it. The figure is actually based on the volume of the ship, and not easily explained.

To put it very simply, the dimensions of the ship are measured and its volume is calculated. This volume is then considered in terms of the weight created by passengers, crew, furniture, fittings, baggage, food, fuel, and other items that could be crammed into it.

My little mind imagines that the 227,000 tonnes is actually a combination of the true weight of the ship, plus the weight of the theoretical maximum cargo.

The physical weight of the ship is not important when the ship is stationary, but when it moves it actually moves a similar volume of water. This is known as displacement.

4

So, when you watch a giant cruise ship, or oil tanker for that matter, moving gently down the Solent, there is hardly more than a small wave created. Unfortunately what you don't see is that several thousands of tonnes of water have been parted by the ship's bow and hull and pushed to the side as it moves. As the ship progresses, this water returns to where it came from behind the vessel.

This action is a little bit like a giant sink plunger that pushes away, and sucks back the water like an invisible tsunami under the water. It creates a pressure wave radiating downwards and outwards from the ship.

The result for Venice is that the downward pressure wave churns up the mud, and the outward pressure wave crashes into the foundations at the side of the city's canals.

You have seen the destruction caused by earth quake tsunamis, and although not as serious, a ship is still producing a shock wave with thousands of tonnes of water hammering into the quite fragile structure on which Venice exists.

So as our floating paradise sails down the canals of Venice (some of which are a mere ten metres deep) it sucks up and circulates tonnes of mud. At the same time the waves push tonnes of water towards the banks, smashing into the buildings and their foundations.

The city is in a continual state of being repaired, but where does that repair money come from?

An obvious solution should be the Venetian port authorities who raise vast sums of money by charging the ships to dock. Although difficult to get an accurate figure, I have read that the cost of docking a cruise ship could be in excess of $10 per passenger. So if we consider the 2016 passenger numbers, it would result in revenue of $15.5 million, or around £12 million.

Unfortunately it seems the city of Venice misses out on this revenue, as apparently it goes straight to the Italian government.

The city only benefits from what the passengers spend in the shops, cafes and bars. If I make a very conservative estimate that each passenger spends £10 on their visit, the revenue is about £15.5 million per year. Now, that is going to produce a significant tax income for the city, but still not sufficient to make the very expensive repairs to underwater foundations of the unique buildings.

A plan was to be implemented in the year 2014. It would force cruise companies to restrict the numbers of vessels of over 40,000 tonnes, and completely ban ships of greater than 90,000 tonnes passing along the scenic waterways to the present cruise terminal.

6

The people of Venice rejected this plan and allowed cruise ships to continue unrestricted.

The reason for the rejection was that no suitable alternative route was currently available to the dock, so the number of visiting cruise ships would have been slashed. That does not mean that the problem can be ignored, and sooner or later something will have to be done to reduce the damage.

Just to complete the story, here are a few tonnage figures for some possibly familiar ships.

Fred Olsen's 'Braemar' is a mere feather at 24,000 tonnes, while Saga's 'Ruby' is 24,500 and P&O's 'Adonia' boasts 30,000 tonnes. A little heavier, and exceeding the magic figure of 40,000, and hence in the class of ship that was to be restricted, there is Thomson's 'Majesty, at just under 41,000 and Fred Olsen's 'Balmoral' at 43,500.

Looking at some of the biggest ships that would still be able to sail along the Giudecca Canal come P&O's 'Oriana' at just over 69,000, 'Oceana' (77,500), 'Aurora' (76,000), and 'Arcadia' at 83,000 tonnes.

Just into the list of the gigantic vessels that would have been banned, are Cunard's 'Queen Victoria' at 90,049, and 'Queen Elizabeth' at 92,000 and the first of P&O's giants 'Ventura' weighing in at 116,000 tonnes.

There are many more floating hotels (or perhaps more accurately floating holiday camps) that would have similarly failed the seagoing obesity check for Venice.

The long term solution appears to be opening up new routes along less glamorous canals to the current terminal, but maybe a new terminal is required. Something has to be done if Venice is to remain a favourite with cruise ships.

So if you are glancing at brochures or online offers for a cruise to Venice, perhaps you should decide quickly, to avoid missing out on one of the most sensational sea going experiences on offer. To help you make up your mind I thought I would describe the relaxing journeys our cruises have given us, and the delights that Venice has to offer its visitors.

Sit back and enjoy this delicious gourmet meal of adventures from our cruises to the beautiful, historic, and unique city of Venice.

Why A Cruise?

A lot of people (in fact the majority) who want to visit Venice will jump on an aeroplane one morning, and a few hours later will leave the plane in the warm sunshine of Italy. This is without doubt the simplest, quickest, and most painless method of travelling the 700 or so miles to Venice.

......*unless of course you are terrified of flying*

So now you know why I am talking about the use of a cruise ship, rather than starting the story with my arrival at Venice's Marco Polo airport.

Apart from my morbid phobia of flying (sometimes referred to as aviophobia), I believe that a cruise has other reasons that might make it more appealing.

Firstly, a very big benefit of a cruise to Venice, is that the trip will almost certainly also call at the historic port of Dubrovnik, either the day before or the day after. It's a mere 300-mile overnight sail between the Venetian port and Croatia. These two cities make a very special package, and rate highly on the *'must see before I die'* locations.

Unlike stories of airport delays, ships are usually waiting at their berth, ready to leave on time as scheduled. Even with the worst weather that the Bay of Biscay can dish out there is rarely a delay to a ship. Apart from problems following a refit, I have never heard of a ship being so late that it could not be boarded at Southampton as planned. Hence delays are almost unheard of, and trust me, there is a far smoother check-in process.

Secondly, you can take as much luggage as you can squeeze into your car. There are no limits for a ship, and you don't even have to move it any further than taking it from your car's boot, as the porters take it off your hands as soon as you stop at the terminal. An optional parking service also takes your car away for secure parking, and this is often free nowadays with a cruise.

Finally, and more importantly, a cruise is not just a way of getting to and from the destination. The journey becomes a part of the holiday experience. For those people who still have a busy job, the first couple of days at sea allow you to switch off from work. And when you turn left at Gibraltar, the sunshine and warmth of the Mediterranean is usually guaranteed, and allows the holiday proper to begin. At the end of the holiday, those final two days gently allow you to come out of holiday mode and prepare to return to work. This is what I found for ten years, and my colleagues often remarked on my ability to settle back into work better than the flyers.

Deb (my wife) and I stumbled on cruise ship holidays with a special one-off trip for our silver wedding anniversary……we have never looked back.

After three years exploring the Western Mediterranean and the Canaries we decided the annual trip in 2003 would be to Venice. Already addicted to the P&O fleet we booked on the MV 'Adonia'. This particular vessel only stayed with the fleet for a short time, and a major reason for us choosing her was that the pricing policy allowed us a first chance of having the luxury of a balcony cabin.

So, on 18th June 2003 we boarded the good ship Adonia on a voyage to Venice for a 17-day holiday that opened our eyes to this wonderful city.

The Starter Course

(The Outward Journey)

Explore the ship and make yourselves at home

+

Sip a cocktail in the Bay of Biscay

+

Make friends and smile a lot

+

Mediterranean Medley of Spanish and Italian delights

+

Relax in the sunshine

The Holiday Begins

If we assume that the cities of Dubrovnik and Venice are the main courses of our gourmet holiday, then it is worth considering the pre-dinner drinks and hors d'oeuvres as time that can be enjoyed on the trip down the English Channel and then across the Mediterranean to the Adriatic.

It takes between two and three days of sailing to get from Southampton to the Mediterranean Sea, and yes it can sometimes be uncomfortably rough, especially in the Bay of Biscay. However to put it into perspective, in the 30 or so times we have crossed this area, it has been calmer more often than rough. If, like me, you are prone to sea-sickness then don't let it put you off a cruise. I have felt sick maybe four or five times but a little white pill took away the discomfort on all but two occasions. I have been all around the world, and survived hurricane-force gales in the Atlantic and tropical storms in the Pacific without a problem, and it was only when I forgot to take a pill in time that my stomach finally gave up.

On our first voyage to the Adriatic it took six days to get to Dubrovnik. Going down the English Channel gave us a chance to explore and enjoy the facilities of 'Adonia'. She was quite new, with glitzy décor and lots of space on the decks and in the public rooms inside. Our cabin was large and the balcony was a real treat which allowed us to relax and enjoy the sunshine in our personal space, or to just hang over the rail and watch the ever-changing water go by.

The first evening on board is always an adventure, finding the dinner table and meeting our new friends who would dine with us for most of the next seventeen nights. Our dinner-mates proved friendly, and we had wonderful conversations each evening as we enjoyed the delicious food and superb service from our pair of waiters. As with all the ships we have been on, we quickly felt at home as we made the most of our time enjoying the atmosphere, bars, and entertainment.

By the third day we had entered the Mediterranean Sea and the sun was pleasantly hot. During that morning there was an event to remember as 'Adonia' was joined by her sister ship 'Oceana', while a helicopter took some promotional video footage as the two ships sailed side by side.

Deb and I were sunbathing by the pool. We did a lot of that during the cruise but this was the first really hot morning. It is usually quiet while at sea with just the throb of the engines, and the chatter and laughter of the passengers. While lying in a state of deep doze, the sound of a different engine attracted my attention, and looking around the sky to locate the source of the interruption to my meditation, I spotted a helicopter.

It was only a little helicopter and, thinking it was just a pleasure flight for someone, I was prepared to accept

14

its intrusion, but then I became intrigued to see a door
was open on one side, and someone was sitting there
with a camera pointing down at 'Adonia'. Deb was also
fully alert by now and asking what was happening,
together with hundreds of other passengers whose
concentration on sun-worship was being disturbed.
Rather than just a fleeting visit to take some pictures, it
became apparent that our visitors were flying around us
taking video footage from all angles. Some people
waved, others grumbled, but most were questioning
what was going on.

After a few minutes of confusion, the alerting *'bing
bong'* of the PA preceded Captain Rory Smith making an
announcement that initially just pointed out the bleeding
obvious; we were being filmed. Fortunately he then
added a bit more detail, telling us it was for a
promotional film and that if we looked to our starboard
side we would spot 'Oceana', our 'twin' sister ship. We
would be sailing alongside each other for a little while at
a distance of about a quarter of a mile as the helicopter
gathered as much footage as possible.

The ship was wide awake now, with unusually
energetic passengers rushing to crowd any vantage point
on the side, to firstly spot 'Oceana' and then to realise
that a quarter of a mile is actually quite close. We could
even see her passengers waving to us, and although we
couldn't make out their words, we could hear shouts

from passengers like ourselves. Soon there was a multitude of strange but fruitless two-way conversations that we knew were happening, but without any comprehension of what was being shouted back and forth.

After about 30 minutes the Captain made a further announcement that 'Oceana' would be breaking away and turning around to resume her voyage back towards Southampton. The helicopter took its final shots, and as the two ships sounded their horns, total strangers waved goodbye to each other across the sea, and very quickly we were alone again and turning towards the coast of Spain.

The resulting video was called 'The Twin Sisters', but the project was not the best planned idea as Adonia returned to the Princess Line after less than 18 months in the P&O fleet. We have a copy of that video (now converted to DVD), and along with the others collected over our early years of cruising, it occasionally comes out on a TV-barren Saturday evening to help us remember and smile at the ship, and the wonderful voyage we enjoyed on her.

Life on 'Adonia' quickly returned to relaxing in the sunshine, and the buzz of excitement quietened as the morning moved towards lunchtime. Around midday the ship arrived in the port of Malaga for an afternoon visit.

16

Malaga was a new port for us but we hadn't booked an organised tour as Deb had done some research about the city, and our plan was to go and look around the Alcazaba Palace. As well as being a palace it is also a Moorish hill fortress that overlooks the city and the docks.

Almost as soon as we had finished lunch and the all-clear-to-go-ashore was announced, we grabbed the usual bits and pieces and strolled into the city towards the fortress entrance. This was the first time we had ever been brave enough to do our own thing on a cruise. It involved getting to, and paying the entrance fee, for the site. We had some initial concern about talking to the ticket seller, but we needn't have worried as he spoke enough English to shame us. This fortress and palace is quite imposing, with tall stone walls and an entrance that is at the top of a hill. Apparently it is reckoned to be the best preserved Moorish palace in Spain.

Once we had made the walk up the hill and gone through the gate into the fortress we were amazed to find a quite special place. Unfortunately a lot of the detail of our visit has been forgotten, because for the only time in all the years we have been on cruises, the camera batteries went flat and we have no photographs to bring the memories back. So the best I can do is to summarise the things that have stood out after ten years.

17

I do remember the tall imposing walls which blocked out any noise from the surrounding city. We walked along cobbled or paved pathways that meandered around the remains of the original Roman buildings which dated back to before 800 AD. There were a number of smaller walled areas that were presumably houses or store areas in the past, but which were now patches of garden with beautiful flowers and bushes. In one spot there was a Roman water feature with a pond and fountains surrounded by pillars and arches. In other places there were examples of the different peoples who had invaded the city and adapted the fortress and palace to their own architectural styles. My knowledge of historical building styles is very limited, but we did manage to loiter and overhear some of the tour-guides giving snippets of information to their groups.

Being high up, there were terrific views from the wall at numerous look-out points, and we could see the dockside and our ship, as well as horse-drawn carriages taking tourists for a trip around the city. One unusual sight was a stadium for bullfighting, which may disgust the British but has always been very popular in Spain.

We survived about an hour in this intriguing place before the lack of cover in the heat of the early afternoon sunshine became too much. We made our way back to the streets below where typical Spanish planning provided some shade in the narrow streets. As

Deb and I made our way towards the city shopping area
we passed the imposing Cathedral with its high walls
towering over a garden area with cats snoozing in the
peaceful cool spot. No matter how hard Deb and other
British cruise passengers tried to attract the cats'
attention, they ignored us.....perhaps they didn't
understand the language.

By the time we found the major shops we realised
that the majority of the Malaga population was now
enjoying their daily siesta and having lunch in air-
conditioned homes. Most shops that might have been
interesting to us were shut, so window shopping was our
only option. In the end we made the most of a Spanish
afternoon and had a cup of coffee while we sat under a
huge parasol watching the small number of people not
resting.

As we sat and gazed around us there were one or two
locals but several tourists wandering past us, and the
song about *'Mad dogs and Englishmen'* sprang to mind
as I realised just how hot it was becoming. Sadly by the
time the Spanish returned to work after their peaceful
lunch period we would have been exhausted by
exposure to the heat, so we gave up our exploration of
Malaga and returned to the ship's air conditioning.

After just three years of holidays in the
Mediterranean sun I was already realising why a siesta is
so popular and necessary in the heat. The problem for

19

the British is that we see and feel the hot sunshine so rarely that we cannot resist its brightness and warmth. Since experiencing hotter countries, I was beginning to see the benefit of taking a break from the sun at lunchtime knowing that it will still be there in an hour's time, and most probably again tomorrow.

Back on board 'Adonia' we had a cooling drink or two and took advantage of the sunshine, knowing that if we became too hot our cool cabin was just a few minutes away. By late afternoon all the passengers were back on board and the ship slipped away from Spain for an overnight journey across the Mediterranean to the Italian island of Sardinia.

By the next morning we had arrived at the southern end of Sardinia, and the capital city of Cagliari (it seems that the 'g' is silent). We had planned before leaving home to save our tours budget for the cruise highlights at Dubrovnik and Venice, so we were going to do our own thing again today. The plan was for a walk around the city and look for a souvenir or two, but also to try and see a Roman Amphitheatre that we had learnt about in the port talk.

We had our breakfast early in the buffet while the ship was docking, and were soon ready to go ashore for a walk. It was already hot at 9:00 in the morning and the forecast was that it would rise to near the 30°C mark as the day wore on. Having been caught out by unexpected heat in the past, we went prepared with drinks and sun hats as well as a liberal coating of sun protection cream.

The city was architecturally stunning with lots of beautiful buildings, and tonnes of marble. There were also picturesque squares to relax in while watching the Italians going about their daily business. Many of the locals laughed at the cruise ship tourists as they gazed at maps and pointed in seemingly random directions at street names.

Our target was the amphitheatre and we quickly found the road and walked slowly up a hill with hopes for a special treat.

When we arrived at the entrance to the amphitheatre we struggled to understand the signs, but deciphered enough to know that it was not open to the public today. We later found out that it was closed while they prepared the venue for a stage-show. The place was surrounded by quite a tall hedge but we managed to climb it enough to get a glimpse of this Roman masterpiece. The workmen were building a stage and erecting lighting and audio systems, but we could just about make out the slope of the hillside with its stunning 1800-year-old limestone seating.

It had been a bit of a wasted walk but we felt a sense of achievement that we had found it, and at least saw a tiny bit of it.

21

We walked back down the hill to the shopping area where we found something to bring home to remind us of the day, together with a bottle of coca cola to keep in the cabin fridge for the hot days to come.

It really was hot by late morning: we were wilting, and it was time to get out of the sun. We were also beginning to feel peckish, so having been away from food for a couple of hours, we strolled back to 'Adonia' for a spot of lunch.

With full tums again we found a spot on one of the decks to resume our worship of the sun, while making the most of the cocktail waiters to keep us hydrated...

.....wonderful!

The next day was a sea day, and late in the morning the Captain announced that we were just about to pass through the busy shipping lanes in the Straits of Messina. This is the narrow channel between mainland Italy and the island of Sicily, and ferries constantly crisscross the area. Along with the additional problem of dozens of small fishing boats it becomes seriously hazardous. It was like the maritime version of Piccadilly Circus, but the Captain and pilot got us through safely with just the occasional use of the ship's horn, and not long after lunch we had returned to full speed on our way north-eastwards toward the Dalmatian coast of Croatia.

The afternoon routine was maintained with a restful few hours in the sunshine, interspersed with cooler moments on our shaded balcony with a chilled glass of coke. As usual, late in the afternoon we showered and went to the individual quiz to challenge our minds (just a little) and enjoy a beer or a glass of wine. We never over-indulged at that time of day as dinner was quickly upon us with delicious food, good service and a catch-up chat with our dinner-mates.

In the evening we enjoyed a show, and then watched the ballroom dancers in the 'All That Jazz' show-bar for an hour, wishing we knew how to waltz and quickstep. With our nightcap over we took to our beds knowing that when we woke up the next morning we would be approaching Dubrovnik in Croatia, to begin the Main Course of the cruise.

Alternative Starters for those first few days

Another benefit of cruising is that although the main destinations may be the same, the ports that are visited on the way there and back are usually different. So if you have enjoyed a cruise to Venice and would like to go there a second time but don't fancy seeing the same ports during the journey, fear not.

One of the delights of cruise holidays (well with P&O anyway) is that even if you take the same basic cruise two years running, there will almost certainly be some different ports to visit. We have been to Venice several times and the places we have stopped at have rarely been the same.

Just to give you a flavour of these differences, here's a brief overview of the ports we visited on the other holidays where the Adriatic gems were the priority.

+++

July 2007 – 'Arcadia'

We loved Venice so much after that first visit that it was inevitable that we would eventually book on another cruise to that superb city.

......hence in July 2007 we boarded the MV 'Arcadia'.

24

'Arcadia' was almost brand new, and although this was our first time aboard her she quickly became one of our favourite ships. She is still in service with the P&O fleet, and like 'Adonia' she caters for adults only. I have to make it clear that this was not our reason for choosing her.

Other than the lack of children, a very noticeable feature of the ship was the older age profile, with an abundance of mobility scooters and walking sticks.

We actually chose 'Arcadia' because it was going to the right place at the right time for us.

Slightly bigger than we had been used to, 'Arcadia' was similarly decorated to 'Adonia', with lots of glitzy chrome and glass. As well as internal lifts throughout, she features lifts with panoramic views on the outside of the ship, allowing the less squeamish passengers a chance to watch the sea as they move from deck to deck. There is a delightful swimming pool area at the stern end, and since a refit it features a large space where hundreds of passengers can quietly enjoy the views, or join in with the occasional lively deck party under the stars, and dance the night away.

By this stage of our cruising experiences we were choosing balcony cabins as a standard requirement, and 'Arcadia' offered the largest cabin (in our price range) that we had ever had. To be honest we have never been disappointed with cabin sizes on any ship, but this one gave us significant extra space.

Anyway, Captain Ian Walters commanded her on this trip and we set off down the English Channel. During the afternoon Deb and I found our way around the ship before it was time for dinner in the Meridian Restaurant, with the usual perfect service and food, plus the company of four friendly table-mates. The outward journey started with one of the calmest crossings of Biscay we ever experienced, so we quickly relaxed into our annual holiday.

The second night on board we had the customary 'Welcome on Board' cocktail party. This is when passengers dress in their finest, and get the opportunity to meet the Captain and some of the other officers, while making the most of free drinks from the generous waiters. Over the years we have perfected our attendance at these 30-minute parties and we always try to chat to an officer with a good number of gold stripes on his shoulder. The waiters pay more attention to these officers, and hence you get more drinks.

Early in the morning on the third day we arrived at our first port which was Cadiz in the southern Spanish province of Andalucia. The city is perhaps 100 miles west of the Straits of Gibraltar and the Mediterranean. It is believed to be the second oldest city in the Iberian Peninsula, founded around 1100 BC. Perhaps a little

26

more interestingly, Cadiz has a very special place in British history as in 1587 Francis Drake besieged the city and sank a great many Spanish ships. The event is remembered as 'The Singeing of the King of Spain's Beard'

On a previous visit to Cadiz we had enjoyed an organised walking tour around the city, so we knew how easy it would be to wander and enjoy ourselves without getting lost. 'Arcadia' was only in port for the morning, so plenty of time to do our own thing again.

The port of Cadiz is very cruise ship-friendly, with just a couple of minutes' walk to the dock gates that open directly onto a road, and once across it the popular sights of the city are within a few minutes stroll. Very quickly we came to the imposing 'Monument to Cortes' with a tall stone pillar that is guarded by a pair of stone horses and their riders. The monument was built in recognition of the first national 'Cortes' (Spanish name for the governing assembly), formed in 1812. Down below the pillar is a symbolic empty presidential throne to signify that a president was no longer in charge.

In front of the main sculpture there is an 'Eternal Flame' burning. This is such a common sight throughout European cities.

With photographs taken we walked around the monument to where there is a small park giving the already dehydrating visitor a chance to sit and sip some water before moving into the narrow streets that crisscross the city. Many of the streets have shaded residential properties with flowers growing in pots on their balconies. Elsewhere the streets provide a vast shopping choice, with some dedicated to fashionable outlets while others concentrate on souvenirs or perhaps the day-to-day needs of the population. Of course there are plenty of cafés and bars to tempt you, and we had visited one of these (called La Cava Taberna Flamenco) on a previous visit to Cadiz where we were treated to a show of Flamenco music and dance.

At the end of the streets you often come to a small square, or Plaza, where there always seems to be a fountain, and crowds of tourists enjoying the peaceful atmosphere while staring at the architecture. Some years before, we had stopped at such a square to have an ice cream and saw a local man gently pick up a weakened pigeon and dip its beak in a fountain to allow it some refreshment. A great number of us stared in amazement at such a simple gesture of humanity.

On this particular visit we quickly moved on to the Plaza de la Catedral where we had sight of the cathedral with its tall towers and impressive golden dome, that can be seen from all over the city, and even several miles out to sea as well. Here in the busy square at the bottom of the entrance steps of the Cathedral there were various street theatre acts to entertain us, and a market to buy souvenirs. We had an ice cream (yes another one) while watching the people of Cadiz enjoy the sunshine just like ourselves. No more than a few minutes away from there is the city's museum with art and architecture on display. The museum never appealed to us, but for some this is a *'must not miss'* place.

With some time remaining, we continued onwards to the waterfront on the other side of the city from the docks. This was a chance to stroll along the wide pavements while staring one way to sea and the other at the remains of the city wall, and the delightful mixture of old and new buildings of Cadiz.

This was just a short morning visit, but for those who were not familiar with the city and wanted something other than architecture and shopping, there were organised tours on offer. Nearby are small villages that allow the visitors to see and sample the quieter traditional life. Jerez de la Frontera is where tourists can taste the local sherry (Jerez), and a little further away is the hillside village of Arcos de la Frontera. These small villages are magical experiences, and regular visitors to Cadiz head for them to avoid the commercial 'sameness' of the city.

We had seen enough, and bought a few souvenirs, so we made our way back to the dock and had a rest in our air-conditioned cabin on board Arcadia.

After lunch we sailed away and a strong wind started to blow across the ship as we moved out to sea. By evening we had made our way into the Mediterranean, with the lazy prospect of two full days at sea before our scheduled arrival in Dubrovnik.

Although the wind that we encountered as we left Cadiz did not appear to have any effect on 'Arcadia', it stayed with us all the way across the Mediterranean.

+++

June/July 2009 – 'Arcadia' (again)

At the end of June 2009 we joined 'Arcadia' again for our third voyage to the Adriatic. The ship had become a real favourite by now.

It was the same ship, the same Captain (Ian Walters), and the same eventual destination, but the outward journey was different again.

The journey south was very smooth and on the third day we arrived in the Spanish port of Almeria, which is a little over 100 miles further east than the Mediterranean city of Malaga. Although we had briefly stopped here before, we had not explored beyond the town, so this time we booked onto a tour that was to take us to the mountain village of Mojacar (from its Roman name 'Mons Sacra'). A lot of tourists go to the coastal resort suburb of the town, but we were more interested in the whitewashed houses clinging to the side of the mountain.

Like so many Spanish villages, it is a delight to visit Mojacar. It has refused to bow to the pressure of tourism and kept the buildings as they were designed to be. Coaches can't enter the main parts of the town, and with a very small parking area they tend to drop passengers off and then disappear until required again some hours later. Yes there were a few private cars and delivery vans, but essentially the narrow roads between the houses were quiet.

Our guide took us along alleyways with terracotta pots hanging on almost every whitewashed wall containing cacti plants, or better still spilling beautiful flowering trails of geraniums to please the eye. The houses sometimes left their ornate wooden doors ajar so we could admire their tiled floors and carved furniture, whilst others had gates to small courtyards with lazy cats and dogs asleep in the shade.

We had a short stop at some Roman ruins which also had a lot of Moorish influence, before arriving at a small square. It was dominated by a pretty church that was explored by many people on the tour. Those of us with less faith, stayed outside in the square where a waitress was quietly setting up tables and chairs at a café shaded under a flowering tree. It was too early for a drink yet, but I am sure many were tempted back there later. This was so peaceful, and apart from the chatter of our group the only sound was the trickle of water coming from a pure white stone fountain depicting a statue of a lady water-carrier.

Our tour took us further up the hillside to an area called Mirador del Castillo which is the highest point of the town. From here we had views of the town itself and also further afield across the barren desert-like landscape that we had driven through on our journey earlier. This area of Spain was the setting for many of the Spaghetti Western films such as 'A Fistful of Dollars' and 'The Man with No Name'. One of the tours from 'Arcadia' took passengers to a set of a cowboy town used by the film crews. Not that interesting to me, but a lot of people enjoyed it.

After returning down the hill to the main square (Plaza Nueva), the guided walking bit of the tour was over and we had time to explore the shops, or in our case have a delicious cup of coffee with a small doughnut to dunk, plus the attentive company of a tiny sparrow that we shared our cake with. Deb and I sat outside the café in the warm sunshine and we had the same wonderful views out over the desert that we saw from the top of the town. This was a really beautiful and peaceful little place and I recommend a visit here no matter how you get to the area.

Souvenirs bought, and more ice cream eaten, our coach returned and took us back through the barren dry landscape to the port of Almeria and our floating hotel. From our balcony we looked out over the port to the Alcazaba Fortress on the hill above the town. It dates back to the first century AD and was used by the Moors, Muslims, and Christians as they made their way across the European continent. We haven't visited the fortress (so far) but several passengers gave very positive feedback about the place.

Organised tours from the ship took people to wander around the Alcazaba while others looked at the Cathedral and the Museum (Museo de Almeria) that has an exhibition of prehistoric relics from a nearby region called Los Millares.

We were more than happy to relax on the ship while others braved the glare of the sun.

Almeria had given us a chance to stretch our legs for a few hours, but by the early evening 'Arcadia' was on the move again with another two days at sea across the Mediterranean, then through the Straits of Messina and north to the Croatian coast.

+++

May 2011 – 'Aurora'

Moving forwards to May 2011 and we have the 'starters' course for our most recent trip to Venice, aboard 'Aurora' that we spent a lot of time on during 2011 and 2012.

The Captain was David Pembridge and we were trying out the grade of cabin (sorry 'stateroom') that we thought we would be occupying on our world cruise just eight months later. In reality we were given a cabin upgrade for our exploration of the planet, but we didn't know about this until the last moment.

Anyway we set off again on the 21st May with a different style of outward journey, with three stops before the main course arrived.

On the fourth day out we arrived in Palma on the Spanish island of Majorca or Mallorca to the Spanish. It was hot and it was sunny, and as we had been here on numerous occasions we skipped the tours and went for a walk around this familiar city.

The one thing that visitors can't avoid stopping and staring at is the imposing Cathedral, which stands across a busy road from the waterfront where the shuttle buses drop off their passengers. Its conception was in the year 1235 at the request of King James 1 of Aragon but it was not completed until 1601.

......certainly a good contract to get if you were a stonemason in that era

The main cathedral building is truly magnificent with a multitude of different sized towers, and it is huge giving it an enormous internal space.....not that we have ever gone in to see it.

To make it even more visitor-friendly, the Almudaina Palace was built right next to the cathedral to give tourists a second place to explore without walking more than a few paces. This palace started as home to the Moorish rulers but as with many such buildings it changed hands over the centuries and became the residence of the Mallorcan kings.

Deb and I have wandered around the external areas of these buildings on several trips, and there are some wonderful photographic *"aaahh"* sights around each corner.

Having crossed the busy road from where the bus stopped, the first feature is a huge lake with water features and statues to please the eye and camera lenses. Once the lake has been investigated you carry on and come to a paved area where you can be entertained by street theatre. Each time we have been there several people have been dressed up (and made up) as statues, monsters, or film characters, and stand on a box perfectly still until an unsuspecting child comes to poke the supposed stone structure, at which point it comes to

35

life. The performers are truly amazing considering they stand motionless in the hot sun for hours on end.

Moving closer to the cathedral, there is a shady corner with a small pond where we used to see a pair of black swans swimming and amusing us. Sadly these wonderful birds have disappeared on our more recent visits. The next visual treat is a long and narrow tree-lined water feature, with fountains that project up and across the feature like a living tunnel to thrill the visitors. Birds sit and bathe in the water or forage for food along the pathways and flower gardens to the side.

What I have described is all before you get to the steps up to the cathedral and palace that proudly wait to be admired by thousands of tourists each week. We pay homage to this area each time we arrive in Palma, but quickly move on to the commercial area to treat ourselves to so many other memorable sights.

Almost everywhere you go there are squares with cafés around the outside, or perhaps an open-air market to investigate. If you get too hot, there are escalators or stairs that take you down to an underground supermarket or another small stall market. We have bought several souvenirs in one such market, including some of my favourite wooden boxes which I collect on my travels.

Up to street-level again, and there is an imposing building that is the administrative centre for both the city and the island. It is bedecked with flags of the country and province, and has armed guards to show off its importance. Very close by are examples of Gaudi architecture that we first saw in Barcelona many years ago, but which still bring a smile to our faces. This area of Palma (known as the Plaza de Cort) has one other memorable feature which is a giant 100-year-old olive tree with a gnarled trunk that dominates and shades a corner where visitors and locals sit and doze.

For those who want to see more of Palma or the island, various organised tours are available, but on our many visits we have only ever had a scenic ride of the city on an open-top bus. The only other thing we have considered is the little land-train that continually thrills tourists with slightly bumpier and rustic rides, and whose clanging bell brings a smile to most passengers.

Once again, a short stop to stretch our legs was all that we wanted from Palma. So with fresh stocks of coca cola for the cabin fridge, and another ice cream eaten, we headed back to relax on board 'Aurora' for the afternoon.

That evening we left Mallorca and continued our journey eastwards across the Mediterranean Sea. Overnight we passed Sardinia to our north and then turned south towards our stop in Sicily. By the next morning we had sailed around the Mediterranean's largest island and arrived at our next calling port of Catania on the island's east coast.

We had been to Sicily before but so far had never stopped at Catania on our travels. This meant we chose to have a tour which was going to the small town of Zefferana, a few miles to the north of our landing point. This is a hillside town in the shadow of the island's infamous volcano Mount Etna, which was gently smoking as it snoozed a few miles away.

Zefferana may be small, but it can make you smile in delight at its narrow streets between rows of architecturally stunning houses. Some have the country's flag proudly draped over their balconies, but just as likely it would be their clothing drying there. Stroll around the corner and there are squares with gardens featuring fountains and marble statues to excite the camera shutter fingers.

Our tour spent a few minutes at one of these squares which was dominated by the cathedral and also had the extra treat of an ornate town hall at right angles. Opposite this building there were steps leading down to a garden area with places to sit and enjoy the sun as well as a superb fountain. The cathedral entrance is up a number of steps with mosaic patterns in the stone and flanked by rows of pots with flowering shrubs and small bushes to brighten it up. The town hall has steps as well, but these were clean white marble with statues guarding the approach to the flag-bedecked entrance. The stop here was a lovely few minutes to explore the cathedral or to just make the most of the nearby photogenic scenery.

From Zefferana we moved into the countryside and up into the nearby hills. We were shown the end of a lava flow from Etna's 1992 eruption, and our guide enthusiastically pointed out a building that had been destroyed by the eruption, and then just a few metres away another that had survived as the flow came to a standstill. The local people celebrated the end of the eruption by building a monument, and it is obvious that it gets a lot of visits, judging by the amount of flowers around it.

Our coach took us further up the hill to the main attraction of the tour. Recently created with views of the volcano, it was a family-owned vineyard. The 'Vivera' is farmed organically and had only just started producing wine. Its enthusiastic owners wanted us to see and enjoy what they had created and we were one of the first groups to visit them. The owners' daughter took on the role of guide, and she started by showing us some young vines that looked very small and vulnerable in the lava-strewn rocky landscape. Next we came to rows of older and mature plants that appeared far stronger and more comfortable, proving that the volcanic soil is very fertile.

Moving inside, we followed the wine's journey past the currently empty storage areas for the grapes, followed by the crushing equipment, then past the stainless steel vats with their computer-controlled environmental systems to ensure the best possible wine. There had been very little to impress us so far, but the bottling plant was a little more interesting to see, with people completing the process as they packed boxes with the bottles. We remained polite throughout the tour, asking questions of our obviously proud guide who was showing off her English skills as well as a love for her job.

Finally we arrived in a large hall with tables covered in samples of the wine plus a wonderful spread of local cheeses, olives and bread. Our smiles probably gave away that many of us had been waiting for this moment, and we happily tucked into the food and small glasses of the different wines available. Of course many people bought bottles to take home, and I am sure the family made enough money from these sales to cover the cost of the wonderful spread of food.

The tour had been a really good mix and I think most of us came back with happy memories, full tums, and a slight alcoholic glow.

Late in the afternoon 'Aurora' set sail again, moving eastwards to cross the Ionian Sea for our next stop.

The following morning we awoke in the peaceful setting of the Greek island of Cephalonia. This was a new place to us and it looked as if the island was also quite new to the cruise industry. With no room for a traditional harbour-side terminal, they have built a concrete road on reclaimed land out to a series of concrete piers. The main one is large enough to deal with the comings and goings of the passengers, as well as allowing the ship to be serviced with fuel and water from tankers. This main pier is connected by steel walkways to a couple of other smaller piers that allow the ships to be tied up securely. From the shore the ship almost looked as if it was at anchor in the bay, with the concrete areas just a little higher than the water level.

Our mooring spot was at the island's capital town of Argostoli, in the south-western region where a third of the population lives. There were mountains creating a beautiful backdrop to the town, and several tours were available to visit attractions such as caves and lakes as well as scenic views of the island. Many simply took a transfer to a nearby beach and enjoyed the superb weather.

We, on the other hand, had no desire to do anything special, so took a walk into the town to look around and enjoy our usual ice-cream and coffee while we looked for a souvenir or two. It was obvious that the area had only just started down the cruise-tourist trail, as although the town was beautiful, there was little to persuade us to spend money. Along with several of 'Aurora's passengers we took a ride on the little motor-train, and as we turned each corner the driver enthusiastically blew a whistle and rang a bell to announce the arrival of tourists to the sleepy Greek population. We laughed and waved as the locals stared at us in amazement, but there was little (at that time) to look at or capture our imagination in the town. There was one moment of excitement though, as a small group of flag-waving protesters marched along the road. The group was creating quite a stir with the town's people, but they caused us no problem and we left without any idea of what their protest was about.

Soon we were back on board 'Aurora', relaxing on our balcony and enjoying the sunshine of this tranquil spot. We had used our stay at this port to gather ourselves for the next couple of busy days, before arriving at the highlights of the cruise in Dubrovnik and Venice.

Main Course

(The highlight ports)

Feel at home on the ship

+

Choice cuts of Historic Dubrovnik delights

+

Tantalise your taste buds with a helping of magical Venetian landmarks

+

Relax in the sunshine

Dubrovnik

With our taste buds tantalised by the delightful cruise across the Mediterranean with visits to a selection of ports, it was time for the main events of the holiday. The Adriatic ports of Dubrovnik and Venice were most peoples' favoured ports for the cruise, so the following pages will reflect on our experiences.

I start with the first visit and our first cruise to the area on board the wonderful 'Adonia' in 2003.

+++

After a night sailing north across the Adriatic, our cruise brought us to the port of Dubrovnik on the Dalmatian coast of Croatia. All the ships we sailed on berthed in the relatively new part of this very famous city, at the cruise terminal of Port Gruz. Some ships anchor in the bay of the Old Town and tender their passengers to and from its historic harbour, but this is an experience that we have not yet had.

As we made our final approach towards our berth we were instantly amazed by the view of a huge road bridge, known as the Franja Tuđmana Bridge, that carries the Jadranska Highway over this waterway. It is an imposing backdrop to the port, with a waterfront that was quiet but quite busy with yachts that occasionally sailed (well, motored actually) past the ship. Back in 2003 the people on these yachts looked at our ship in awe, but as the years have gone by, more and more money has come into the Croatian economy, and the local rich no longer have much interest in the ships that help to fill their tills.

Another memorable sight that first morning was the number of young people swimming in the crystal clear water, with many people playing water polo, which is a major sport in this country.

On all of our visits to this port we have visited the historic Old Town of Dubrovnik, either as a part of an official tour, or using the shuttle bus to take us there from the cruise terminal. Even this short ride has changed over the years. We were welcomed with smiling faces a decade ago, but now the immigration and customs officers are quite likely to inspect every coach, and insist on seeing everyone's passports. The traffic has also increased from being a busy journey in 2003 to utter chaos during our last couple of visits.

In 2003 we booked a P&O organised tour which took us by coach from the dockside through the streets of the commercial areas of Dubrovnik to the Old Town. Our coach dropped us off just a couple of minutes' walk away from the fortified walls. Our tour guide described what we would be doing and gave all the usual warnings about staying together while we were being shown around, and to take care of our possessions.

The start of our tour was a guided walk through the Old Town. Even entering was inspiring, as we crossed a bridge over a moat before passing through the Pile Gate (just one of its two enormous gates) that allows entry through the huge defensive wall that surrounds the town.

The first thing that greeted us as we entered was the huge domed 16-quadrant circular Onofrio Fountain and Cistern. It was built by Onofrio Della Calva in the fifteenth century to celebrate the completion of the new waterworks supplying the town from a river 12 kilometres away.

It's no longer functional after being severely damaged in an earthquake, but its stone seating around the outside is popular for weary travellers to rest and rehydrate with a drink while they watch the hundreds of people passing by.

The Old Town only has a small population actually living there, but each day the numbers swell by thousands from early morning till late at night, all enjoying the charm and history of Dubrovnik.

As we got our bearings our guide pointed out a building to one side of the cistern that started life as a Franciscan Monastery. Over the years it became the

Pharmacy and it is preserved in that state and is now open to the public as a museum. It was a pleasure to go inside where it was cool compared to the oppressive heat that this part of the world subjects to unsuspecting tourists from the cold wet shores of Britain.

Like so many of the tours, this one was a very quick-moving experience and we were soon outside again walking along the main street called the Placa. The street is paved with blindingly-white marble slabs, and has shops and cafes on either side. Every few metres there are small alleys running off from the main street that lead up to the hill above the city on one side or deeper into the backstreets on the other.

Placa Street is the place to walk, and to see and be seen. It is obvious that many of the people visiting here are dripping in wealth, and show off the obligatory designer labels for every item of clothing and accessory being worn or carried. Cruise ship passengers aren't regarded as being special enough for any attention, and are often seen as nothing more than a supply of cash. Fortunately you don't have to be a celebrity or wealthy to enjoy the sights and sample the culture and atmosphere of this incredible place.

Our walk continued to the end of the street where we had a glimpse of the beautiful harbour. Our guide realised that many of us wanted to spend some time here, and let us know there would be time to do our own thing after she had finished the look around the rest of the town. Coming away from the harbour we passed the Church of St Blaize, and then were given a chance to look inside the Cathedral of the Assumption. There were also whistle-stop looks at markets and other noteworthy streets before we arrived back at the cistern where we had started. We were now given thirty minutes to wander around by ourselves, and we quickly retraced our steps to the harbour to soak up the atmosphere of this pretty little waterside tourist trap.

We had a fantastic 90 minutes in the Old Town of Dubrovnik and were already hooked on its atmosphere, history, and architecture. A mental note had been made that Dubrovnik had to be added to the *'very special places to return to'* list.

During our time in the town, our guide gave us a history lesson and pointed out some of the major landmarks from the siege of the early 1990s. There is a map of all the building showing which ones had been damaged by artillery attacks, or more astonishingly the rare ones that had not been hit. Shell holes are still visible to remind the short memories of tourists just how bad it was for the town's population. Dubrovnik is now a UNESCO World Heritage site and serves as a warning to the world of the conflicts that killed so many, and left even more with physical and mental scars.

From the city we re-joined our coach and went on a drive around the local countryside. This included a stop to look down on the Old Town from the cliffs above. With the island of Lokrum in the distance, the view down over red tiled roofs, narrow streets, enchanting harbour, and the fortified wall, all appeared even more amazing, and cameras worked overtime catching memories.

The stop was short as there was much more to see, so it was back onto the coach.

During our drive we saw more evidence of the war, with empty houses where the occupants (with the 'wrong' religious beliefs) had fled the army. Many of the houses were destroyed and just a burnt-out pile of rubble, but others looked to be in perfect condition externally but had no-one living in them. Someone asked the guide why nobody was living there, and her reply was so simple and to the point.

"They don't belong to us".

The guide explained enough to make us realise the pain and anger that still exists, but without going so far as to make listening to her difficult.

Soon we arrived at a village called Uskopolje for a traditional Croatian lunch at a beautiful taverna-style restaurant. The restaurant was situated next to a trickling stream with a waterwheel and a long table shaded under huge parasols and overhanging trees. It was a wonderfully relaxing time, and a chance to chat to our fellow passengers. The food was sometimes mysterious but generally delicious, and I didn't hear any complaints from the normally '*very picky*' P&O passengers.

Suitably refreshed we moved on again to the nearby fishing village of Cavtat. This quiet and pretty village is situated in a little bay with a pebble beach, and a small harbour where local fishing boats bobbed up and down. We followed the road around the harbour where there were shops to investigate and cafés for those who wanted a drink, as well as lots of places to just sit and look at the water.

For a few minutes we sat on a wall looking at the world passing by, before dipping our toes in the clear and cold Adriatic Sea. While we soaked up the atmosphere we watched more people playing water polo. Its popularity was obvious, with grandstands on the shore looking down on the area where the sporting youngsters enjoyed themselves.

Cavtat was a delightful little village, and after an ice-cream it was time to get back to the coach and our journey back to the harbour and our ship. This had been a delightful day with friendly people and breath-taking scenery. I didn't hear a single bad comment about our tour, and more importantly, about the truly wonderful experience of Dubrovnik.

Late in the afternoon 'Adonia' was unhooked from the Croatian dockside and we glided quietly away from the harbour and back into the Adriatic.

+++

July 2007 – 'Arcadia'

After that first visit to Dubrovnik we promised ourselves that we would go back, and two years later we were in the Adriatic again aboard 'Arcadia'.

We were up early for an expected arrival in Dubrovnik just after breakfast. Ready for a quick getaway, we sat high up in the ship in the Crow's Nest with a wonderful view ahead of us. Sitting with us was a Scottish couple that we had made friends with, who were as excited as us for the day in Dubrovnik.

I began to be suspicious as our expected arrival time was 8.30 but it was that time already and our view was a very distant one of the cliffs. Before it became totally obvious that something was wrong, the Captain came on the public address system to announce that due to the windy conditions we had suffered since leaving Cadiz, we were very late arriving

We were very aware that it had been windy but we had no idea it had been so bad to make us this late.

51

Captain Walters continued his announcement by telling us that he had been discussing the situation with the P&O head office in London for some time, and he now dropped the bombshell that a decision had been made that 'Arcadia' would not make landfall at Dubrovnik on this cruise.

.....there were groans all around the ship

Many people had booked the cruise because of Dubrovnik being on the list of ports, and our Scottish friends were devastated. Having been there before, our situation wasn't quite as bad, but it was a serious disappointment.

The Captain apologised and explained that there were still a couple of hours sailing time before we would have arrived at the port, leaving very little time for the visit. He went on by saying that Croatia was still a very suspicious country with overzealous rules that prohibited entry into their territorial waters unless the ship was going to berth, so he could not even give people a 'sail-by' of the city.

When you book a cruise, the small print clearly states that changes to venues may occur due to circumstances beyond the control of the company, and the weather is often a culprit. There was no alternative but to change back into sea-day shorts and t-shirts and relax in the sunshine. 'Arcadia' had now slowed down and was making a leisurely trip across the Adriatic towards Venice.

Nature provided one coincidental bonus……the wind dropped and it got even hotter!

+++

June/July 2009 – 'Arcadia' (again)

Two years later, and we were up early once more, and this time we had no problems from the wind and would be docking as planned in Dubrovnik.

Our arrival went very smoothly and we could see that the harbour had changed quite a bit in the four years since our last visit. There were more modern buildings on the quayside, and the yachts had become longer and shinier as the Croatian economy had blossomed.

Our plans had been made for several months: we intended to take the shuttle bus to the Old Town and then simply walk around the walls. We were off the ship reasonably early and on board one of the first shuttle buses.

This is when we noticed the first of the changes in attitude of the country.The border guards stopped the coach at the dock gates and came on board to check us out. It was nothing more than a glance at us but the smiles had gone.

The delay was minimal and we were quickly on our way again. We now saw another sign of the country's improving financial situation with far more traffic on the road, and it was virtually a nose-to-tail trip to the bus stop at the gates to the Old Town. We were in no rush so we didn't mind.

We had a wonderful morning. Our early arrival at the gates meant that although it was busy with tourists, the major rush had not yet started. Tickets purchased at the steps to the wall walk, we climbed up the narrow pathway and the view that greeted us was just breath-taking.

In most places the walkway is wide enough for people to pass comfortably, but occasionally the route narrows, mainly because of damage, making it a little congested. To one side of the pathway we could look inwards to the city over the red-tiled rooftops and the numerous church towers and domes, plus the narrow streets and gardens below. On the other side was the wall perhaps a metre wide and just a little more than a metre above the cobbled path.

Our initial view over that wall was of the road we had walked down to the Pile Gate, and also a small rocky bay with a tiny beach and one or two fishing boats. Looking a little to the left there was a cliff with a fortress on the

54

top and just a glimpse of a garden area with trees behind it. Directly below us we could see the drawbridge we had crossed where there were now hundreds of tourists slowly making their way into the Old Town.

As well as the sounds of people chattering, there was a busker on the seating area of the cistern in the square below us, playing a strange musical tune on an even stranger instrument. It was a stringed object looking vaguely like a balalaika but played with a bow, like a violin. There were very few changes of note being scratched out by the old man, resulting in his performance being little more than a short repetitive melody. He was enhancing it a little by stamping his foot on a hinged wooden box arrangement to tap out a beat. For a couple of minutes the sound was eerie, and slightly interesting, but as we started our walk we could still hear the scratching and clonking that had no variation, and it grew increasingly painful to listen to.

.....I hummed that tune in my head for many hours.

Anyway, our wall walk was amazing as we strolled anti-clockwise around the town. The view out from the town changed to the sea, and the steep walls led down to the rocks with occasional flat sun-trap areas for visitors and locals to enjoy the warmth. There were several places where the more adventurous sun-worshippers could climb a little further down to dip their toes into the clear water.

Every now and then our pathway widened, and small lookout towers with arrow-slot windows reminded us that this was a fortified town that repelled invaders for hundreds of years. We spent a lot of time just leaning on the wall and staring out to sea as ferries and fishing boats passed by on journeys in and out of the old port. Another delight was a fleet of little yachts that sailed by us in a line, with children being taught the art of sailing.

Rather than just concentrating on the sea views, we also spent a lot of time looking inwards to see the day-to-day lives of the Dubrovnik's inhabitants. Many of the yards, or small gardens, had a washing line of clothes drying in the intense heat, and most had cats or dogs sleeping in the rare shaded spots. There were rarely any signs of the occupants, who could have been out shopping, or perhaps working in the shops and cafes, or maybe just relaxing behind the shuttered windows.

After about 15 minutes we started to meet walkers coming the other way, making our path a little more congested. You can get onto the wall at the two gateways at either end of the town, and we were now seeing those who took the other way up. The pace of our walking was quite slow, and several family groups who were perhaps finding the walk less interesting than us, had overtaken us, but now we had to be careful in the narrowest sections with the two-way traffic.

When we reached the half-way point there was no option but to return to ground level as there was a gap in the wall at the harbour. The sunshine had been quite intense and there was very little shade on the wall, so this seemed the ideal opportunity to get an ice-cream and a cold drink while we spent a few minutes in the old harbour area. It is also a wonderful place to sit and watch the boats and people. Water always attracts people, and the cafés were doing a roaring trade with drinks, and there was a good number of visitors being tempted to sample the local food, either as a late breakfast or an early lunch.

Our short rest from walking was over, and we climbed back up the steps to the top of the wall to continue on.

We were now on the inland side of the town overlooked by the Srd Hill. If you are wondering, "Srd" is apparently pronounced as "Serge". This hill has a cable car taking people to and from the top where there is a fort that was a lookout during the troubles. I don't like cable cars so I have never been interested in taking a ride up there.

This area of Dubrovnik outside of the town wall is dominated by modern housing, with a large number of villas and small hotels for tourists, and does not make the most attractive view from the town walls. Of course there were still magical views down onto the red-roofed buildings and the shaded alleyways or narrow lanes that crisscross the Old Town.

After two hours of walking we were at the highest point on the wall, and nearly back to our starting point. We took our final photographs before carefully descending the steep steps back down to the square. The old man was no longer playing his monotonous folk tune.

It had been a delightful morning but we were now very hot, and very tired of walking. After a few minutes looking around the shops we had had enough and made our way out of the town, to catch a shuttle bus back to our air-conditioned ship, and lunch. By now traffic conditions were chaotic, and made worse by the arrival of a second cruise ship that was now spilling her passengers into the Old Town area. There were a few minutes of frustration and confusion as we waited for a shuttle bus assigned to P&O, but eventually we settled into our seats in the comfortable cool bus for the ride back to the harbour and 'Arcadia'.

Had we had enough of Dubrovnik now?

.......no, we were already making plans to come back and walk the wall again in the other direction.

+++

May 2011 – 'Aurora'

Our trip across the Adriatic was calm and warm, and quite early in the morning of 29th May Captain Pembridge had successfully secured Aurora alongside the harbour at Dubrovnik. Our plans for the day were simple: jump on a shuttle bus when we were ready and go back to the Old Town, where we would repeat the walk around the wall, but in the opposite direction to last time.

With breakfast over, we had our wash and gathered our bits and pieces together for our morning's adventure.

Security had got even stricter over the previous two years and this time we had to take our passports with us. At the port gate the border guard not only came on to the bus, he looked at each individual person's passport. This is not a complaint about the level of security, I am just pointing out that there had been a lot of differences in just eight years.

Now, we had been warned repeatedly about needing our passports, both by tannoy announcements and in the ship's newspaper. So why on earth did one couple have to embarrass themselves (and the rest of us) by not just forgetting their documents, but moaning loudly when they were ordered off the bus and told to return to the ship. We can all make mistakes, but we don't compound it by arguing innocence.

The rest of the passengers mumbled under their breaths (yes, we did too) but we were given the all-clear and allowed out into the Croatian streets on our way to the historic Old Town.

Well the wall walk was as good as we hoped it would be, and we were continually spotting things we had missed the first time. Perhaps our walking pace was a little quicker, and perhaps there were fewer stops for photographs, but as we descended the steps at the end we had no doubts that it had been a worthwhile morning. This time we finished our morning with a good look around the shops and markets. We also relaxed at the harbour to soak up the atmosphere and watch the comings and goings. Today was busier than we had seen before, as the normal fishing and sight-seeing boats were sharing the water with lifeboats from a Costa cruise ship, that was anchored out in the bay and transferring hundreds of its passengers to and from the shore.

The weather was superb once more, and having refreshed our minds with the wonderful sights of Dubrovnik's Old Town, we made our way back to 'Aurora' and soaked up the warmth and sunshine for the remainder of our stay.

So what else could we have done, if we had wanted to stimulate our minds a little more?

Tours available from the ship included a wide choice of trips or activities for curious passengers. One tour looked at the region from a boat that was just a little smaller and closer to the water than 'Aurora'. We could have paid a visit to a Croatian village to soak up the culture of village life in the countryside. Another trip took passengers to the countryside again, but with the emphasis on experiencing the local food and drink. Many passengers enjoyed trips that were similar to our first visit with the fishing village of Cavtat being a favoured destination, as well as the region around Dubrovnik.

I'm confident that if you are planning a trip to this wonderful place that you will find something to make you smile, make you think, and probably make you want to return.

Many people come to Dubrovnik to experience the history of the distressing siege and bombardment by Serbian forces that the town suffered during the war-torn years of the early 1990s. I remember the footage on the television with the white-suited reporter, Martin Bell, letting the naïve people of Britain see and hear about the horrors facing civilians in that sad area of the world. There was a reminder of that television news coverage on our cruise as the guest speaker was Martin Bell (still in his white suit) who gave a wonderful talk interspersed with video clips of those bulletins. He is now an unofficial ambassador for the city of Dubrovnik and exudes knowledge and real passion for Croatia and the war that killed so many, while splitting up communities who had lived side by side for decades.

Coincidentally, he was also on the early part of our world cruise eight months later, where he repeated this and other talks, and thrilled many of the passengers again. We didn't go and listen to him on that cruise, but we often saw him wandering the decks in the sweltering hot sunshine in his immaculately clean (if a little creased) white suit.

As we sailed quietly out from the modern port of Dubrovnik that evening, we leant on our balcony rail watching some of the expensive yachts and power boats passing by, as we made our way out from the sheltered waterway into the Adriatic, for our overnight passage to Venice.

I think we have satisfied our hunger to see and experience this place, but without a shadow of a doubt, if the opportunity arose to come here again I think we will jump at the chance.

Venice

Returning to our adventure in 2003, we had now been on our cruise for over a week. We had thoroughly enjoyed the beauty of 'Adonia', relaxed in the warm sunshine, and seen the wonder of Dubrovnik. Now it was time for the star attraction: the city of Venice, sometimes lovingly referred to as '*La Serenissima*' (the most serene) by the locals.

The magic of the arrival to Venice starts many miles from the city, as the ship follows a deep water channel from the Adriatic through the outer lagoons of the city. The route is marked by buoys which guide large vessels safely, and a pilot assists the Captain on the bridge. The pilot has navigational control of the ship during this and most entries to a port, but the Captain retains command. To be honest, for the majority of ports around the world, the Captains could perform the required manoeuvres perfectly adequately, but protocol has to be respected.

All the arrivals that we have experienced to this Italian city have been early morning, and often before it was fully light, but the thrill of Venice always tempts hundreds of passengers out of their beds. They are up on deck, sometimes with jumpers and jackets to protect against the unexpected early morning chill, and leaning on the ship's rails at every available observation point. Around the world there are a number of ports where almost everybody gets up early to experience a special arrival, and Venice is one of them.

So on Thursday 26th June 2003 we were at the forward end of 'Adonia's highest public deck to get the clearest view, and our first glimpse, of this Adriatic gem. On this first visit, the sun was already warm, and we glanced from left to right as the port lecturer gave a commentary of our arrival, and directed our eyes towards different landmarks such as the small patches of land, canals, and buildings that we passed. Getting closer to the centre of the city we started to see the most recognisable tourist spots, but Venice is more than a collection of buildings, it is a completely different sort of city.

It's difficult to appreciate that Venice is not part of the mainland, nor is it an island that has a rivers or canals passing through it. This is a huge lagoon with occasional shallow areas of water that have allowed patches of land to be created, or to have wooden piles driven into the mud to support buildings. It is a man-made site reclaimed from the sea, and without a lot of continual effort and money it will eventually return to nature, as the wooden foundations rot.

As I mentioned at the beginning of this book, the cruise ships are making the situation worse, as they daily churn up the mud and make waves that hasten the destruction.

Back to our arrival, and we were still in the deep water channel carefully making our way along what is in effect the watery main road to the city. Every few metres there were small narrow canals joining the waterway, with little bridges for pedestrians, but it was impossible to capture every stunning scene on camera. By the time I had spotted and pointed the lens at a bridge, I would be distracted as a water taxi, or a waterbus (known as a Vaporetto) came into view with the passengers shouting hello and waving at us. Fortunately it didn't matter about missing a delightful example of a stone-arched bridge, as another side canal and an even more stunning bridge would quickly appear, with more early morning Venetian commuters waving to us. Even though there is rarely a day without the arrival or departure of a cruise ship, the majority of the local people increase the magic with their enthusiastic waving and greetings. I quickly got a sense that they really loved their city and proud to live in this fairy-tale land, but they were still happy to temporarily share it with holidaymakers each day.

Noticeably the smiles and gasps were increasing as we moved towards the main built-up area of the city, at the intersection of the Grand Canal, and Giudecca Canal. As we got closer to St Mark's Square on our right, people whispered things like 'Bridge of Sighs', 'Basilica', and 'Doges Palace'. Then fingers pointed and cameras clicked as the first of the gondolas was spotted. These beautiful, sleek, black boats are universally recognised as an iconic symbol of Venice, and like many others I had an instantaneous desire to be relaxing in one with Deb, while being serenaded by a gondolier, as we quietly made our way along a secluded canal. There were several surreal moments as the hundreds of passengers on deck would seemingly be struck dumb as Venice revealed each different delight from its box of magic for us to see.

Deb and I were almost drunk with pleasure at seeing so many famous landmarks, and so many beautiful new sights in such a small area as we relaxed on our floating hotel. Time was temporarily forgotten, but as we approached the berthing area at 8:00 am we realised we had to get some breakfast. Soon it would be time for our organised walking tour of the wonderful city.

Our walk started just a little way from the dockside and would give us a chance to see the backstreets (or back canals) of Venice with its wonderful architecture, while our guide gave us a history lesson and some amusing anecdotes. The houses with their faded pastel-coloured walls were generally built three storeys high to provide shade against the summer heat. Most had small balconies whose main use appeared to be for hanging washing. As extra protection from the hot sunshine, most of the windows have wooden shutters across them.

We saw numerous churches and many had tall towers allowing their bells to be heard across the city. Without warning we would turn a corner to find tranquil squares where the locals sat in the shade discussing the state of the Euro, the price of fish, or maybe the ever-increasing numbers of tourists. There were often ornate fountains and cisterns that could have once been a part of the water supply for those living nearby, but which now had become a feature for tourists to photograph. Within a few minutes of our walk the peacefulness was very noticeable, with the only sounds being birds and our guide whose powerful voice could have been heard a long way off.

He named and described the squares, churches and pointed out buildings with stories or of special importance. One of his many jokes has always stuck in my mind when he was talking about the Italian language that few of us understood. He said there were two Italian words that all British people understood: pasta and Mafia.

I would hope that his generalisations about the British lacking knowledge of the language were slightly inaccurate, but his remarks were very close to the truth in my case. On a more positive note, over the next few years Deb and I went some way to addressing this weakness and took evening classes in Italian. Although I still struggle with an Italian talking at full throttle, I do have a basic knowledge of some of the words and how to phrase a sentence.

An obvious delight of the walk was turning a street corner and finding a canal. Every few minutes we would be crossing them over arched bridges that gave us all a chance to see the busy life of these waterways. You can assume roads are non-existent in the majority of Venice that tourists visit, so all services have to be via the water. There were delivery barges stacked high with fruit and vegetables, then others carrying furniture and cardboard boxes of who-knows-what. The refuse was similarly transported from each little collection point beside a canal and taken away. Of course there were gondolas full of smiling visitors who were sometimes being serenaded by a musician or the gondolier singing. But they were not the only transport options, as water taxis like speed-boats took the rich and famous to and from hotels, and on the larger canals there were vaporetti water buses that service the general public.

Of course there were other water-craft that are not seen quite as regularly but which are vital to the city. An occasional police boat and ambulance passed us going significantly faster than most other crafts, with blue flashing lights and two-tone sirens. We never saw one, but there are fire boats as well and these are important in a city where most buildings are made of wood or standing on wooden piles. We saw a wedding couple and their guests on the way from a church, and we even saw a funeral boat. That was one of the few moments that I switched off my video camera as soon as I glimpsed the black feathers on the prow of the barge.

After an hour or more strolling through the quiet areas we arrived at the busier Grand Canal, and the atmosphere changed. It was noisy and the water was no longer still, but bubbling with the traffic passing by continually. We visited the daily fish market, although being quite late in the morning it was not as busy as perhaps we expected it would be. The slightly less than fresh fish were beginning to make my nose twitch.

Before we left Britain, a lot of supposedly knowledgeable people had warned us that it was not a good idea visiting Venice in mid-summer, as the city stinks!

Whenever anyone has suggested this to me in the years that followed, I have been quite adamant that I didn't find any such smelly conditions anywhere, except for the fish market. Yes the canals do not have clear water, and suspicious trickles of something seem to be pouring into them at regular intervals, but having been there four times, and always in hot weather, I have never found it to have any disagreeable smells.

Our guide was now making our smiles even broader with the beautiful and well-known sights he was showing us. There was the Rialto Bridge over the Grand Canal with steps up to its shops and viewing points down to the canal. It was crammed with people all soaking up the atmosphere and capturing the scenery in this oh-so-special city. We quickly joined the crowd there, and below us we could see cafés with hundreds more tourists sipping their ridiculously expensive cappuccinos and looking up at us on the bridge. Gondolas, water taxis, vaporetti and private boats streamed by below us with many of the occupants waving at the cameras as they passed under the bridge. The scene is as spectacular as it is beautiful and cannot fail to amaze the newcomer, and yet it still brings a smile to the most regular of visitors.

We had to be dragged away from there as our time with our guide was over. He took us back to where we had started and we returned to 'Adonia' for a rest and some lunch, but we were going back into the city as soon as we could. With all the cruises we have done there is always an assumption it might be the only, or last time, we visit a particular city, so we do our best to make the most of our time wherever we go.

With lunch over and our bodies rehydrated, we bounced down the ship's gangplank on our way back to the city to look at the touristy bits we had not seen that morning. This time we bought tickets and took a vaporetto, and we were soon splashing along in our waterbus alongside the local Venetians, and feeling rather proud of ourselves for trying to do our own thing.

Our plan was to get off at St Mark's Square, and that shouldn't have been a problem as we knew what it

70

looked like. The journey took us down the major
waterway running alongside the Giudecca area and
every now and then it turned into the side at the various
stations.

Now in Italian, 'St Marks' is known as 'San Marco' so I
kept my eyes on the names as we approached each stop,
and eventually spotted the name 'San Marco' so grabbed
Deb and we returned to dry land once more.

*.....unfortunately there is more than one Vaporetto stop
which includes the name 'San Marco' and I chose the
wrong one.*

Chastised gently by Deb we soon sorted ourselves out
and discovered how simple it is to find your way around
Venice. There are numerous signs high up on street
corners that help tourists by pointing the way to the
major landmarks, and it was not very long before we
came out of a small side-street, and St Mark's Square (or
Piazza San Marco) was in front of us.

The same wise people who warned us of the bad
smells in Venice, also insisted that the square would be
packed with tourists, and a total waste of time.

....wrong again!

Yes it was busy, but there was plenty of space to walk
around, and using our own guides and maps we quickly
identified the buildings around the square. The
architecture is stunning, and panning around us we

71

gazed at the Doges Palace (Palazzo Ducale), Cathedral of St Mark's (Basilica di San Marco) and the tall bell tower known as the Campanile di San Marco. Everywhere you look the buildings show off their beauty with different textures and coloured stonework or huge glorious mural paintings. Looking upwards, the roof line is generously enhanced with arches, domes, spires and an amazing clock gleaming in the sun regularly attracting the tourists as it rang out the time.

It is very easy to forget yourself for a moment and sigh out loud at the beauty of this place.

Even the shops and cafés look spectacular, with ornate pillars and columns making the already glorious stonework hide their commercial purpose, tempting tourists to come closer and spend. One piece of advice we received which proved to be correct, was not to use the shops around St Mark's Square as they are much more expensive than the ones in the streets behind. This was true, and we didn't have to look at the prices for long to realise that buying souvenirs or drinking coffee in St Mark's Square is for the rich.......but window shopping is still allowed.

Around the corner we came to what is known as the Piazzette San Marco (or Little St Mark's) from where you can look out between the columns of St Mark and St Theodore to the main waterway, where we had sailed past aboard 'Adonia' several hours earlier. In the dim and distant past public executions took place between these two columns, and some superstitious Venetians still refuse to walk between them.

We bravely walked between them and carried on to the waterside and looked out to where the Grand Canal meets the Giudecca Canal in front of the small Island of St George (Isola di San Giorgio). We turned to our left and, just like thousands of tourists each day, strolled the short distance to look down one of the side waterways towards the Bridge of Sighs. This small bridge, that has some similarities to the Hertford Bridge in Oxford, is where Venetian prisoners would make their final walk from freedom before eventual imprisonment or execution. It is such a small bridge but one that has immense notoriety in history.

With several 'must see' places ticked off our list, we returned to the Square to spend some euros on a visit to the Campanile (or bell tower) of St Mark's. This square tower is some 97 metres high and referred to as 'The Master of the House' by the Venetian people. On the top there is a three-metre statue of the Archangel Gabriel whose wings catch the wind and makes it spin around. There is a lift, but you can also climb the stairs if the queue is unattractive and you have the energy for a significant climb.

Once at the top, the view is jaw-dropping, with a panoramic view of Venice and some distance beyond. I am not a lover of heights but I was glad to have gone up the tower, and looked out over the red-tiled roofs and the numerous churches and other significant buildings. Maps around the observation platform show the visitors what is visible, and helps to put names to the buildings and perhaps make the decision as to where to go next. In the distance we could see 'Adonia' standing proud at its berth, and a young girl standing nearby pointed to it and voiced her amazement to her mother. We kept quiet but felt rather proud that we were a part of a temporary landmark to the city that people were staring at.

Looking down at the square below we had confirmation that it was not crowded with tourists, and there were certainly far more pigeons than people, but perhaps many people were having coffee or a pizza somewhere, rather than strolling around in the heat of a glorious afternoon.

It was time to go back down to earth and we strolled away from the Square and explored the nearby streets with their shops and cafés. One of the most popular souvenirs that tourists purchase is the Venetian mask, that can depict all manner of animals, fictional characters, or mythical creatures. They are made from various materials and come in different colours, as well as being enhanced by all kinds of bits and bobs such as feathers, fur, or glitter, to make them attractive. They also come with a wide range of price tags ranging from

74

ones that a visitor can take away as an inexpensive memory, through to unbelievably beautiful high-quality items requiring serious bank balances to consider them.

I remember we didn't buy one and regretted it afterwards, as the ship had a Venetian themed Ball on one of the formal nights. Instead we bought a couple of small watercolour pictures of the city and a little Murano glass bowl to remind us of our visit.

Midway through the afternoon we were tired, hot and requiring serious rehydration, so it was time to get back to the ship. Once refreshed we spent some time in the sunshine looking around at the sights near the dockside. Just over the fence from our berth there is an old railway terminal. It may not be in regular use any more but at that time it was being used to 'park' some of the carriages used to make up the 'Orient Express'. Even with cruising as my favoured holiday, the idea of a train journey across Europe is still very appealing.

Our stay in the sunshine didn't last very long as a summer storm suddenly erupted around us. It was a dramatically noisy thunderstorm with flashes of lightening and pouring rain. We were lucky as we had moved inside less than five minutes before it created chaos on the ship, with unsuspecting passengers suddenly getting soaked and running for cover.

As is usual with summer storms, within fifteen minutes the rain had stopped and the sun was out again.

It wasn't long before the decks were drying and passengers were making their way outside again to enjoy the return of the hot sunshine.

The ship was not leaving until very late, and many people took the opportunity to have an evening out and a meal in Venice. We had walked so far, and seen so much, that another trip into the city was not appealing. Instead we enjoyed a slightly quieter evening around the ship with several empty tables at dinner. The entertainment was not to our taste either so we just relaxed and stared out from our balcony as dusk gave us a different view of a silhouetted cityscape, before darkness finally took over.

One of the little traditions we have on a cruise is to look around the shops of Southampton during the morning we leave, and to buy a bottle of champagne for a celebration drink at some stage of our trip. This day had been wonderful and everything we could have imagined or wished for, so it was the right time for our balcony celebration. As sail-away time approached we opened our bottle and clinked our glasses and wished for many more cruises to come. At 11:00 pm the stevedores below us set us free from the dock and with a quiet hoot of the horn 'Adonia' moved away.

Suddenly, and without any warning, a firework display started.

We had the naïve thought that it was some sort of celebration for the first visit of 'Adonia' to Venice, but most likely it was the celebratory end to a festival day. Whatever the reason the display was amazing and we "ooh'd and ahh'd" our delight and laughed out loud at the sparkling bursts of colour and explosions. By the time we turned into the main waterway the fireworks had finished and our champagne was gone, so we sat and watched the sights of Venice drift by for nearly an hour. The water taxis and vaporetti purred by and their commuters still waved and shouted to us until we were far out into the lagoon and the city lights were fading behind us.

It was time to sadly concede that Venice was gone and it was time for bed. 'Adonia' was on the way home now, heading south before turning westwards back across the Mediterranean. Venice was a magical place with so much to see and such an atmosphere that we had to have more of it.

The decision had already been made that we would do everything possible to come back again.

+++

July 2007 – 'Arcadia'

It took another four years, but we did manage our return trip, and early in the morning we were up again to watch our arrival into Venice. It was Friday 13th July, and after the disappointment of missing Dubrovnik the previous day, there was a buzz of anticipation around 'Arcadia', as we made our way towards the highlight of the cruise.

At just after 7:00 in the morning we were passing St. Mark's Square and slowly gliding into the Giudecca Canal on our way to the terminal where we would be berthing. The forecast was for good dry weather with temperatures in the early 20 degrees. We had a tour booked that was going to include a ride on a gondola, so we wasted no time in getting our breakfast and preparing ourselves.

The trip started with our group taking a walk along the dockside to join our personal water taxi. This would take us down the Giudecca Canal to the city highlights. Even this simple boat ride was quite special being so close to the water level as we passed 'Arcadia'. We were able to look up at this beautiful ship that was our temporary home. As we splashed our way down the Giudecca Canal our guide pointed out some of the special buildings: one I remember was the Hilton Hotel which apparently was the only one in Venice (at that time) to boast a swimming pool. After perhaps fifteen minutes we turned towards the canal side and got off at a pontoon. From here there was a short walk to where a flotilla of gondolas waited for us.

Each gleaming black boat took six passengers and we were carefully arranged in our seats, and told to sit still by the gondolier to ensure the craft was balanced. One by one the boats set off down a series of quiet canals and the tranquillity of the gentle movements was making us all relax into the magic of the experience. Soon the peace was shattered as we reached the entrance to the choppier waters of the Grand Canal, where it was far busier with other gondolas, water taxis, and private craft.

This was very special, even though we were sharing our gondola with four other people. We were seeing some of the best views of Venice from a vantage point so close to the water that I could dip my fingers in the cool canal. After a stunning view of the Rialto Bridge in the distance we turned back into the quieter waterways again, passing under more delightful arched bridges where occasionally other tourists were watching us and calling out for us to smile and wave, so that they could take photographs.

.....*we had no objection to smiling and waving, this was a wonderful moment.*

Occasionally other gondolas passed from the opposite direction causing our boat to slow a little in the temporary traffic jam. Some of those gondolas just had a couple romantically reclining in the boat while others were fully loaded like us, and one even had an accordionist serenading some Japanese tourists. Sadly he was playing '*O Sole Mio*' but singing the '*Just one cornetto*' lyrics.

After little more than 20 minutes were back to where we had started and being carefully helped back onto the canal side by supportive gondoliers hoping for a tip. It had been a superb experience and it wetted our appetite to repeat the ride.....but on our own.

Once the tour group had re-gathered we sat back in the water taxi again for a further journey to the island of Murano. Here we walked into a factory shop that was organised as a tourist venue with banks of seating allowing us to watch a demonstration of glassmaking.

The show started with a craftsman taking a lump of molten glass from a furnace. This red lump sat on the end of a tube which the artist twisted as he blew into it. In little more than a minute that lump of glass turned into a vase that was streaked with colour from the minerals mixed into the glass lump. The quiet craftsman smiled to the applause he received. Next a similar lump of glass was heated until it started to melt and stretch. The deft hands now twisted and shaped the glass until we realised he was creating a beautiful glass figure of the Ferrari prancing stallion emblem. For the rest of the ten to fifteen minutes we watched and photographed the craftsmen as they blew and shaped the multi-coloured molten glass into other ornate shapes and containers.

We knew this was no longer the high quality and expensive glass that the name 'Murano' once had, but it was stunning to watch a man take a small blob of glass then heat it, blow it, pull bits of it, and bend it until it turned into something that most of us would be proud to display on our shelves.

Demonstration over, we had a chance to look at the factory's wonderful glass creations, including bowls, vases and gold-coloured tea sets, as well as various sizes of the rearing horse. Yes, of course we bought one!!

Back outside in the sunshine we briefly looked at the other souvenir shops nearby, but just bought a delicious ice-cream as we waited until it was time to make the return journey. Our water taxi splashed its way back across the choppy waters of the outer lagoon area before reaching the calmer canal. As we saw St. Mark's Square with the imposing Campanile behind the Doge's Palace, we moved to the left and landed at the Island of San Giorgio for a photo stop, and a look around the stunning Maggiore Church with its white marble frontage, standing on a small chequered-tiled square. Some went inside to look at the church, but like a few others in the group I was more interested in capturing the view across the canal of St Mark's, where it was obviously busy with hundreds of tourists.

Our happy bunch of British tourists returned to the water and we made our way back to the cruise terminal and 'Arcadia'. Our tour was over and it had been a terrific morning. It was time for a late lunch and with our experience-tanks full after our superb morning, we spent the afternoon on board enjoying the sunshine.

Just before 6:00 in the evening Captain Walters announced that we were leaving. 'Arcadia' quietly reversed away from our berth and then turned down the Giudecca Canal with a short blast on the horn to say goodbye to Venice. There was a sail-away party in full swing at the stern of the ship, but we sat on our balcony sipping a glass of wine.

It was not a late night departure this time, and there were no fireworks. Instead we enjoyed sailing past the city as evening approached, with the waterway full of people coming home from work or setting off for a night out. As always, the Venetians waved and shouted to us as we leant on our balcony and waved back. St. Mark's Square was still crowded with tourists, and the arched bridges all seemed to have people leaning on their walls watching us pass by. Our day had been another success and Venice was maintaining its magic for us.

As we sailed out into the quieter areas of the lagoon we spotted the lighthouse that marked the point where we had turned into the Murano area. There was just one last chance to look back at the city skyline and say cheerio to Venice, and we had already decided that we would be back again soon.

That evening we treated ourselves to a special dinner in one of our favourite 'select dining' venues on the P&O fleet. 'Arcadia' had a small Asian-fusion restaurant high up near the funnel which at the time was called The Orchid Room. Our meal was delicious, and we cleared our bowls and plates of the food.

......the perfect end to a perfect day.

+++

June/July 2009 – 'Arcadia' again

This was one of the very special cruises in our sailing history. I don't know why but every now and then things seem to click into place and the world smiles, and this 16-day holiday was one of those moments.

On the 5th July as we made our journey across the Mediterranean we celebrated our 34th wedding anniversary, and the photo taken of us having our evening meal shows a bright-eyed, sun-tanned couple smiling naturally at the camera.

83

Two days later Captain Ian Walters had docked 'Arcadia' at the Venice cruise terminal, and before 9:00 am hundreds of us set off with bulging wallets and itchy camera shutter fingers, to explore the city on a glorious sunny morning.

We didn't have a tour booked, but we had very special plans for the day.

In the previous couple of years we had been taking evening classes to learn some basic Italian, and we set ourselves two challenges. Our first challenge was to ask for a gondola ride in Italian, including confirming the price, and how long it would be for.

The day started with a courtesy shuttle ride on a water taxi from the ship to the landing point near St. Mark's Square. This was our third visit to Venice and, reasonably comfortable with the layout of the city, we set off along the canal side towards the Square. There was a bit of a delay initially, as our arrival coincided with a group of Chinese dignitaries leaving their hotel with an armed escort, and the path was blocked to allow them to safely set off on a personal tour of the Doge's Palace. It was only a short holdup to our plans, and as soon as the Chinese had moved off, the guards melted away and the crowd surged onwards towards the tourist highlight.

We spent a few minutes looking around St. Mark's Square and had the treat of being there as the clock struck 10:00 am, and we saw the figures at the top of the clock hitting the bell with their hammers. This is a major attraction for tourists, and hundreds of us craned our necks to watch the spectacle.

Enough of that, and we set off through the alleyways in search of a gondola.

As we approached one of the little bridges over a canal a gondolier spotted us and gave the rehearsed greeting of *"Gondola ride for the pretty lady?"* I think he was taken aback as we didn't just walk on, and I responded by asking how long the ride was and how much it would cost ......in my best but, very basic Italian.

"Quanto costa un giro in gondola?"

"Quanto tempo sarà?"

He quoted the price and the duration, and from our research we knew he was asking the official price set by the Venetian authorities. We politely declined the offer as our idea was to look around a little before we had our ride. But as we walked off the gondolier chased after us and offered to reduce the ride by 10 euros for the standard 45-minute trip. Without too much hesitation we accepted his offer and carefully climbed into the beautiful boat and snuggled together on the black leather seat. Our friendly gondolier used our camera to take a photo of us, and then another as we gently kissed each other.....yes a couple of typical tourists, but very happy!

It was quite early, and our ride started by taking us along the quiet canals where boats were offloading the daily fruit and vegetables to the cafés and bars. These canals are narrow with just enough room for two gondolas to pass, but there are bends and junctions that hide oncoming boats and we quickly realised that our gondolier shouted a warning "*Ola*" at regular intervals. When a similar response was heard he would slow and move to the side to be ready to pass his colleague when he appeared. Sometimes manoeuvring the long black craft was quite complicated and the skills of these boatmen are amazing.

Our ride moved out into the Grand Canal with its busy and expensive cafés to the side, before we passed under the wonderful Rialto Bridge which was packed with tourists staring down at us. From there our gondola eventually turned back into the narrow waterways and all too soon we were back at our starting point, where we said our thanks and tipped our gondolier for his time.

It had been an expensive 45 minutes but was a magical experience, and worth every euro. A gondola ride in Venice is amongst the top things that people want to do in their lifetimes and I made a mental tick against it with a gold star.

Back on dry land we made our way through the back alleys towards the Rialto Bridge that we had passed under a few minutes before. On the way we perused the shops in search of a Venetian mask for Deb as a very special souvenir memory.

It was time to face my second Italian speaking challenge.

We stopped outside one of the many ice-cream shops and stared at the delicious assortment of soft ice-cream and sorbets. We didn't need to look too closely as it had already been agreed what we wanted. As soon as the assistant came over I cleared my throat......

...... *"Due gelati di lampone per favore"*

In case your knowledge of flavours is limited, I had asked for two raspberry ice-creams. Total success, and after a few moments watching the soft fruity treat being scooped into the cornets we bade a polite "Grazie" (yes most people know how to say thanks) and strolled down the lane with smiles on our faces.

A few minutes later we were standing on the crowded Rialto Bridge watching the gondolas passing below us. Still smiling we sighed with pleasure at the sight we had just experienced. Our delightful morning continued by wandering back towards St. Mark's Square still looking in the shop windows for something to buy. Finally Deb found the mask she wanted and it was a simple but stunning one in silver, with a feather to add a little mystery. It was worn at the next Ball on board the ship and was admired by many.

After a last look at the tourists staring up at towers and mural paintings in the Square we joined a queue to catch our shuttle boat back to 'Arcadia'. We had treated ourselves to a beautiful morning of adventures but it was now time for lunch, and an opportunity to enjoy an afternoon of sunshine on the ship's decks.

The early evening sail-away was as delightful as ever, and we waved and cheered at the water craft that passed us as we slowly made our way down the canals to the Lagoon and out into the Adriatic Sea again. Another visit to Venice was over, but it would not be our last.

+++

May 2011 – 'Aurora'

As things stand at the moment, this was the final time that we got up early in the morning and watched our arrival into one of our most favourite ports in Europe.

There was a mist over the water and the sky was just becoming light as we stood on the observation deck at the front of the ship, and spotted the navigational lights guiding us through the lagoon. Deb and I truly have a soft spot for this city, and although perhaps a little chilly at 6:30 in the morning, we were already smiling in anticipation of what the day would bring.

As is often the case, the ship's port lecturer gave the bleary-eyed passengers a bit of information as to what we were passing, and as we glided closer to the busy Grand Canal entrance there was hardly a space to be found for the late risers to get a clear view of the attractions. That was our cue to go and get breakfast while most people were still outside, and the queues for the food would be minimal.

Our plans for the day were all but zero. We would take our time before getting off the ship to allow those on tours to get off quickly. It would then be a leisurely boat trip to the city centre to look around at the familiar sights and see what took our fancy. We were comfortable with Venice and it was now a place to enjoy a walk in the sunshine.

By mid-morning we were strolling through St. Mark's Square, soaking up the atmosphere with hundreds of tourists from all over the world, staring at the architecture of the buildings, and exercising their camera shutter fingers.

How can anyone not smile and dissolve into happy thoughts in a place like this?

We wandered down an alley away from the crowds and into almost total silence, apart from an occasional bird or the footsteps of a Venetian out shopping. The intense heat reduced as the tall buildings shaded us from the sun, and we noticeably slowed down our walking pace.

There is always something new to discover here. Maybe an ornate wooden door that had survived hundreds of years and still looks wonderful, or a glimpse of a courtyard down a passageway with delightful tiled floors and peaceful cats sleeping after a hearty breakfast. It is rarely more than a few minutes before a canal appears with an almost fairy-tale bridge to cross, or perhaps to stop and look down at a passing gondola, and remember that wonderful ride from a few years before.

After a short while the noise levels increased as we approached the Rialto Bridge over the Grand Canal. For 50 metres around the bridge, brightly lit tourist-trap shops try to attract passers-by to come in, but we simply window-shopped and gasped at the inflated prices compared to what we had seen in the quieter alley outlets a few minutes earlier. Arriving at the bridge itself we climbed the steps to even more shops that tempted credit cards and wallets to be sought from even the deepest pockets to buy a souvenir of the visit, or a gleaming piece of jewellery as a more serious reminder of this place.

We squeezed through the crowds and over the bridge. Rather than buying a souvenir memory we decided to splash out on a cup of coffee in one of the canal side cafes. This was as expensive as St. Mark's

Square but we just had to do it. As we looked at menus a waiter succeeded in winning our custom and we were given a shaded table overlooking the canal with sensational views of the bridge. Yes the coffee was expensive, but this was more than a drink: it was an experience to savour in the long winter nights to come.

The morning was nearly over and we took our leave of the Rialto area and returned to the narrow alleys. Rather than going straight back to 'Aurora' we had decided to stay in the city a little longer and have a pizza for lunch. After reading some menus and discussing if a café looked suitable, we chose one where there were a few locals eating, but which was not too busy. I don't remember what flavour we chose but we had a pizza each and quickly realised we should have had just one and shared it. But we overcame the size issues and devoured the delicious food. Temptation got the better of us and we also had a cake to finish off our lunch.

Slightly bloated but distinctly happy we paid the quite reasonable bill and thanked the owners. Off we strolled again down the narrow streets in the direction of St. Mark's Square. After taking a final look at the Doges Palace, the Campanile, and the general hustle and bustle of the Square we jumped on the courtesy boat back to the cruise terminal, and spent the remainder of the day enjoying 'Aurora's sunny decks.

This had not been a visit where we had any burning desires to do things, see places or buy anything special. We like Venice, and we enjoy the atmosphere of both the busy tourist traps, and the peaceful areas where life goes on as normal. We are content to look around and absorb what the city has to offer, and there are lots of things that we can do....if we get the urge.

Just as with many of the cities of Europe that we have visited over the years, there comes a time when the thrill is to enjoy the ordinary aspects of a place rather than to get a buzz from a particular building, factory, or museum. As we walk around Venice there are always new shops to check out, cafés to tempt us and thousands of people to watch. There are simple pleasures such as sitting in a quiet square with an ice-cream watching old ladies shopping, or young mothers discussing how their children are growing up. At other times it can be fun to get near to a group on a tour and listen for a moment at what the guide is saying, and watching the look on the faces as they are amazed by the information that is being imparted.

There is always a café where a cup of coffee and perhaps a little cake allows us to chat, and consider what to do next, and of course sometimes a pizza with a glass of red wine lets us feel just a little more at home in this wonderful city.

That evening we sailed down the canal again and waved goodbye to a city that is a jewel in the Adriatic. We would certainly come back again if the opportunity arose, but with retirement about to start, the cost of such a cruise may be a little more difficult to budget for. For now we stared around in the evening sunshine and realised that 'Aurora' was taking us on the homeward leg of the cruise. There were still a number of ports to visit, and lots to do on the ship.

…. 'Arrivederci Venice'

Dessert Course

(The Journey Home)

Enjoy the ship to the full

+

Fresh Fruit Salad of Croatian and Greek islands

+

Cheeseboard of Italian and Spanish memories

+

Relax in the sunshine

The Homeward Leg

Our homeward journey was not all about packing and waiting at an airport followed by a delayed flight home to a damp Britain. On a cruise, passengers mentally note that having left the port which is the furthest from home means the ship is heading back, but the holiday continues. The sun still shines, and on these cruises there were several ports of call between Venice and Southampton Waters.

Back in 2003 we gave a sad sigh at leaving the wonderful city of Venice, but we knew there were a leisurely seven days and nights of sailing before we woke up in Britain.

After leaving Venice the good ship 'Adonia' sailed south during the night, allowing any passengers staring towards land a chance to see the off-shore oil wells, whose flames lit up the sky from their platform towers. It is an eerie sight unless you know what it is, but the ship is a long way out to sea from them, so they simply make an unusual distraction from a moonlit ocean when looking over the side of the ship.

Our journey continued the next day as well, and being delightfully hot and sunny most people relaxed from the cultural excitement of the last few days, soaked up the warmth and deepened their tans. For those who preferred something different there was a chance for people to learn a little about Gibraltar from the on-board port presenter, but only a few of the passengers were unfamiliar with that particular place. If exercise was needed then the fitness centre was always there for a run on the treadmill, or to lift some weights, but if that was a little too demanding the daily deck quoits, shuffleboard, and table tennis competitions always had a good following.

Some tried to improve their dancing skills with the professional instructors, while others played Bridge or listened to the guest speaker who was trying to give people advice on making a better quality video of their cruise memories. If the sunshine was producing a thirst there was morning coffee (free in those days) and soon after that the bars opened and life became a pleasant alcoholic haze for many of the passengers.

It was one of the formal evenings that night, with all but the most stubborn dressed in their finery. Entertainment gave us the choice of a song and dance show by the theatre company, or an aging comedian to giggle at in the show lounge. In the Atrium, dancers had a chance to show off their newly-learnt steps, and around the rest of the ship various quizzes exercised the minds at either a fun level, or the dreaded late-night 'syndicate quiz' for the boffins.

This was our fourth cruise and we had by now learnt what we liked to do of an evening, and after watching the show we enjoyed a drink in the Atrium while we waited for a dance we knew, to tempt us onto the floor. In those days we were restricted to simple sequence dances such as a Barn Dance, or a Square Tango at a push, but the frustration of watching people gliding to a waltz rhythm eventually led us to having lessons back home.

Our evening may have ended with a late night cup of hot chocolate and a snack, but it could just as easily been a cup of tea in the cabin with a biscuit, before sinking into a deep sleep to the gentle throb of the engines, and the almost imperceptible movement of the ship as we headed towards our next stop at Messina in Sicily.

So on Saturday 28th June we arrived for our first ever visit to the island of Sicily and the port of Messina. This Italian island is the largest in the Mediterranean and as a geographical guide, Messina is at the north eastern tip of the island at the point that the toe of Italy would kick. It is just about the closest point to the mainland coast of Italy across the Straits (of Messina). We didn't have a tour booked, so we enjoyed a look around the city at its shops, architecture, and fountains. We probably had an ice-cream and possibly a cup of coffee, but many years have passed and the details have blurred.

If we had decided to have a guided tour, there were plenty on offer. One popular trip from the ship went to the pretty little town of Taormina with its hillside location and a Greek Amphitheatre. Taormina lets visitors savour views of the golden beaches below, and Mount Etna close by. Another tour option for enthusiastic explorers combined the walk around Taormina plus a reasonably close-up look at the volcano, and another tour simply spent a few hours discovering more about Etna.

For the enthusiastic historically-minded there was a trip to the Tindari area with its Greek and Roman influences, or if passengers just wanted an overview of the Messina area there were more relaxed coach trips and short gentle walks to occupy the day.

After another day absorbing the warmth and Italian delights, 'Adonia' set sail again and started her westerly crossing of the Mediterranean for our next stop at Palma on the island of Majorca.

It is more than 450 nautical miles between Messina and Majorca, and at a reasonable cruising speed the ship arrived early on the morning of 30th June at the port on the south of the island. Palma is the capital city of the Spanish island known locally as Mallorca, and in 2003 this was our first visit to this very beautiful spot.

Our visit was only for the morning so there was little time for a tour, and many of the passengers (like us) settled for a shuttle bus ride to the centre of the city and a walk around the touristy highlights. It was a glorious morning once again, and with temperatures set to reach 30°C we were careful to take drinks with us. From where the shuttle dropped us off we had a tremendous view back across the bay to where 'Adonia' was moored, and she gleamed in the sunshine.

The bus stopped in a (slightly) quieter avenue just back from a huge junction on a main arterial road through the city. In front of us we could all see the imposing cathedral and the adjacent Almudaina Palace that was the start of the tourist area, but unfortunately that was on the other side of the road. It took several minutes for our group of about 40 passengers to wait for the series of pedestrian crossing lights to give us a chance to get over the highway, but the wait was worth it.

I have already given some detail about the city of Palma, but this first visit made us hope we would come back another time and explore a little more. Having stared at the external architectural delights of the cathedral and palace we walked on into the shopping areas of the city and found a gnarled old olive tree and some intriguing examples of Gaudi's imagination.

In an underground market we found some small shops that sold all kinds of tourist temptations, and this is where I expanded my collection of little wooden boxes. Refreshed by yet another ice-cream we strolled back towards the shuttle bus stop and spent some time in the gardens and lake area below the palace, and caught our first view of the living statues dressed as cowboys or marble goddesses that tempt children to come close and poke them to see if they are real.

It is truly a magnificent city with things to satisfy the demands of most passengers. The history and architecture excite the eyes, and the shops fulfil the retail needs. There are beaches for the seaside lovers, museums to explore, cafés and bars for a drink while you watch the world go by, or restaurants to enjoy a plate of traditional Spanish tapas or paella.

For those passengers who chose a formal tour, there were sight-seeing coach trips of the city or trips to the nearby Marineland Aquarium. Further afield, tours went to the east coast of the island to the spectacular 'Cuevas del Drach' or Caves of the Dragon with their underground lakes. Some people chose to go to the small town of Valldemossa in the Tramuntana Hills to experience more traditional island lifestyles. Valldemossa boasts a 13th-century monastery that has links to the composer Frederik Chopin. I think most people could find something to interest and occupy themselves at this port.

By the end of the morning everyone was back on-board the ship for a late lunchtime sail-away before the

short journey overnight to our final port of
Gibraltar......*and the sun was still shining!*

At lunchtime on Monday 1st July we were tied up
alongside in Gibraltar, and although the temperature had
dropped a couple of degrees it was still wonderfully
sunny. This was just a fleeting visit to the quirky lump of
rock at the tip of the Iberian Peninsula that is a British
Overseas Territory. When the rush to get ashore had
reduced we made our way down the gangplank, and out
through the arrival lounge. Having avoided the queues
and suggestions that we needed a taxi we walked into
the town.

On our previous two visits to Gibraltar we had treated
ourselves to sightseeing tours, one that took us to the
caves and another which was a trip around the bay
looking for (and seeing) dolphins. This time we simply
took a walk down Main Street to look in the shop
windows but mainly just to stretch our legs. I understand
the British mentality that we should maintain
sovereignty of the place as a mark of respect for its
history, but most of the local population sound just a
little Hispanic, and it is no longer a ridiculously cheap
duty-free paradise. Yes it is still cheap for many things,
but to see the numbers of passengers struggling back to
the ship loaded with carrier bags of cigarettes and booze
is somehow just a little bit 'tacky'.

Don't get me wrong, I like Gibraltar as a place and enjoy its atmosphere, history, apes, and the fact that it is often the last stop before the final couple of days sailing up the coast to home.

As usual we bought an ice-cream to lick as we sat in the square and watched the people going by. Long before the ship was ready to leave we were back on board enjoying the relative peace on the decks while hundreds of passengers were eating their fish and chips and downing pints of real ale ashore.

At 6:00 pm Captain Rory Smith hooted the ship's horn and we made our way out from Gibraltar as the sounds of a special British Sail-away echoed from the stern. Entertainment staff ensured there was lots of dancing, flags were being waved and loyal British songs were sung loudly as cocktails, wine, and beer were drunk. This was the final time that the 2,000 or so passengers would experience this party atmosphere on the cruise, and there was fun and laughter but also just a suggestion of sadness that the holiday was coming to an end.

During Wednesday and Thursday 'Adonia' sailed north along the coasts of Spain, Portugal and France including quite a calm crossing of Biscay. We made the most of the weather as the sun said farewell, and then the temperature dropped to that more typical of home. We savoured the final couple of days on this beautiful ship, and enjoyed the evening entertainment. There was one rather special moment on the last formal night when a three metre-high champagne fountain was created in the Atrium. We found a spot on the stairs to watch it being built by the head chef, and then the champagne was poured to the cheering delight of the hundreds of passengers crowding into every available viewing space. Some even used the glass lifts to go up and down continually just so they could see the spectacle.

On our last day there was the dreaded moment when we had to pack our cases, and leave them outside the cabin door to be whisked away by the army of stewards, and made ready for disembarkation. That night we had a lovely dinner with our table mates and said goodbye to these temporary friends. Our waiters were thanked and handed a little envelope with some well-deserved spending money. Before we left the cabin for dinner another similar envelope had been left for our steward.

With the farewell formalities over, we strolled around the ship and remembered the fun of the previous fortnight. There was time for a last late night glass of brandy for Deb and a Drambuie for me before sinking into our bed for the final time.

On Friday 4th July the holiday was over and we got up and saw Southampton from our balcony. It had been a terrific experience and a wonderful ship. When we got home we agreed that we had to go back to Venice and Dubrovnik again.

We never returned to 'Adonia' as the ship moved from the P&O fleet to the Princess cruise line. But we did have a couple of holidays on its sister ship 'Oceana' that we had sailed alongside on our journey out ......and of course we did get back to the Adriatic.

+++

July 2007 – 'Arcadia'

Returning to our second trip to the Adriatic aboard 'Arcadia', let's look at what happened after we left Venice.

Overnight we sailed at a relatively good speed for a 260 nautical mile trip to the small island of Korcula. During the evening Deb and I treated ourselves to a meal in 'Arcadia's Orchid restaurant which is tucked away at virtually the highest point on the ship. This venue specialised in Asian-fusion food, and our meal was absolutely delicious from start to finish. Over the years our cruises on 'Arcadia' have always included a visit to the Orchid restaurant (now renamed 'East') and I personally believe it to be the finest venue on any P&O ship.

Saturday morning, and we were approaching the Croatian island of Korcula. Having missed out on the planned visit to the Croatian city of Dubrovnik, at least this was an opportunity to visit the country. The island has no facilities to dock a ship the size of 'Arcadia' and we were slowing to a halt in the bay around 8:00 am before dropping the anchors. This was a port where the ship would remain offshore, and the passengers taken to land in the ship's lifeboats, that in this role are referred to as tenders. As we got up we looked out from our balcony and saw a very pretty vista with green rolling hills and the red tiled roofs of the town that shared the island's name.

Korcula was a new venue for us and we had booked a tour called "Wines and Countryside". There was an early start, so we couldn't waste too much time looking at the view before getting our breakfast. Soon we were ready to face the world, and fully loaded with sunhats, cameras, money and drinks, we went to the theatre to collect our tickets and await the call to board a tender for the short ride to land.

A ride on a tender boat is a special thrill for most cruisers, as you get close to the water and feel the sea's movement that is rarely obvious on board the ship. Of course, it allows wonderful views upwards toward the ship as well, and cameras were quickly busy capturing memories of 'Arcadia'. Little more than 10 minutes later we were carefully leaving the tender with the helping hands of the crew, to avoid an unexpected swim or bruised legs.

105

With the groups gathered together according to our coloured and numbered stickers, we followed our guides to the small fleet of coaches. Korcula is a small island less than 30 miles long and only about five miles wide, and at the time was only just starting down the path of attracting cruise ships. Hence the island didn't have a lot of coaches but what we saw were mostly of a very good standard. It wasn't overly hot yet but the air conditioning was still appreciated, as we sat and listened to the guide telling us all about the island and what we would be seeing.

It didn't take long to realise how small the place was.

We travelled along a road just about wide enough for two-way traffic, with various factories, farms, shops and views of the countryside. After about 30 minutes we stopped at a tiny fishing port called Vela Luka. Our guide announced that we had arrived at the other end of the island, so we now had a few minutes to walk around the harbour area and buy some souvenirs or have a cup of coffee.

It was a very pretty and peaceful little place.

Deb and I strolled in the sunshine around the waterfront and remarked about the lack of traffic. It made it so pleasant not having to watch out for cars and scooters. As we walked from the car park towards a small cluster of shops we spotted fish visible in the crystal clear water.

106

There were only a few shops and cafés to investigate but we refrained from buying anything. It appeared that most of the objects had originated in China, with no sign of anything manufactured locally. Many of the passengers did their bit for the island's economy and came away with souvenirs, but we hoped to find something more interesting later.

It was time to get back on the coach again and we now retraced our route for a few miles, before turning down a seriously narrow lane and arriving at the small vineyard that was the main attraction for the morning. This vineyard was situated in the Smokiva Valley, and little more than a farmhouse and outbuildings with its wines branded under the name of 'Posip'. The guide introduced us to the family who owned the vineyard and our short tour commenced with a look around the wine-making areas, before we entered the tasting and sales room.

We were ready for the serious business of the morning with a chance to sample some of the different wines on offer, accompanied by nibbles of freshly-prepared local foods. Over the years Deb and I have been to several wine tasting sessions where small plastic glasses are filled with a mouthful of the various wines. They were rather more generous in Korcula. We had full-sized glasses that were refilled once empty, as we moved from red to white. Having found our favourite I think we

107

could have had as much as we wanted. Fortunately we all behaved ourselves and several people enjoyed what they tasted and bought some bottles to take home. Deb and I didn't find the wine overly interesting, but it did loosen our tongues and we had a good chat to our fellow passengers.

Before we left the vineyard we had a wander around the outside of the property, and cleared our heads while looking across a valley to some stunning views of the island.

All that was left of the tour was the trip back to the main town where the guide pointed out some places to look at before we returned to 'Arcadia'. She was very proud of her island and her country and she reminded us of the equally patriotic guide that we had in Dubrovnik on our visit there in 2003. The Croatian people enjoy, and make the most, of their new-found freedom since the civil war.

We spent an hour looking around the city which is split by the main street into two sections. Although we didn't notice it at the time, the side streets on the western side are all straight, while on the eastern side they curve to form a barrier to the cold north-easterly winds. Our aim was to find a souvenir to take back, and we climbed some steps to an open-air market near the cathedral. As the market was busy we walked a little further along the path, until we came to a section of the city's wall with an old cannon pointing out across the water. It acted like a signpost pointing to a spectacular view.

With another couple of photographic memories we returned to the market, and after a few minutes bought a couple of souvenirs that were possibly more local than Chinese. Still experiencing a pleasant alcoholic haze, Deb and I decided we had seen enough of this beautiful little place. It was lunchtime and many of the tourists were settling down in the cafés and bars for some local food and drink, but we felt 'Arcadia's buffet was more to our taste, and a lot less expensive.

With most of the morning's tours now completed, there was a queue of passengers waiting for a tender back to the ship. The wait was pleasant enough as we watched the comings and goings of fishing boats, yachts, and tourist vessels. We were soon back on board 'Arcadia' and went to the buffet to get some lunch. With our tums full we found a couple of sunbeds on the quiet decks and enjoyed the sunshine.

As the afternoon came to an end the Captain made his announcements and the anchors rattled back into the ship, and we set sail again.

The next day (Sunday 15th July) we woke up as the ship was quietly making her approach to the dock of the Greek island of Corfu. Bleary-eyed, our first views from the balcony were of the Old Fortress, followed quickly by the New Fortress or as Deb described it, the Not-So-Old Fortress. This was the second island visit on this cruise, but Corfu was completely different to Korcula. This island is larger and very definitely geared up to attract and cater for the thousands of tourists who arrive here by sea and air each year, to enjoy the almost guaranteed hot sunshine.

After six years of cruising we were now far more relaxed when visiting a port, and we only booked a formal tour when it was a new place and with something special that took our fancy. Our days ashore were more often than not an opportunity to stretch our legs and get a 'feel' for a town or city by looking at the architecture, shops, and the local people going about their normal day-to-day activities.

So this morning we had already made a decision to have breakfast brought to us in the cabin to make the most of our sunny balcony. As we approached our berth we noticed another cruise ship, and we thought it looked familiar. As we eventually docked across the concrete dockside from this ship we saw that it was 'Ocean Village'. This was a vessel which we had sailed on for our second ever cruise in 2001, when it sailed under the name of 'Arcadia'.

.....*yes it was a ship that once had the same name as the ship we were now sailing on.*

110

As we enjoyed our fruit juice, toast and pastries with cups of tea to follow, we watched the activity on the dockside as the two ships offloaded passengers. First those on tours walked away in groups and then a steady procession of couples strolled off towards the port gates. Across the dockside we also saw a batch of pushbikes coming out from 'Ocean Village's hold that were checked and prepared for a cycling tour. Soon the group of slightly more athletic passengers arrived and were welcomed by their guides who ensured everyone knew what they were doing when cycling, plus instructions about where they were going, and what to do if something went wrong. Very quickly the cyclists had put on their helmets and were standing astride their bikes, and after the group had light-heartedly tested their bells, they set off in a long line. Deb had had a cycling tour in Barcelona on one of our earlier cruises and enjoyed the experience very much. I hadn't joined in as I had the chance to go and look at Barcelona's Nou Camp football stadium instead.

With breakfast over, we armed ourselves with maps, cameras, bottles of water and hats to protect ourselves from the warmth of the sun and set off to explore Corfu. Although the island was new to us we decided to simply take the shuttle bus into the town centre, and just be tourists.

111

There was a short walk along the quayside and a stroll along a road leading to the dock gate. Our shuttle bus was waiting just outside and we were soon on our way. It dropped us off at a parking area just outside the Old Fortress that we had seen as we arrived. A representative pointed us in the direction of the town which we could see on the other side of a large grassed area. Apparently this is the only cricket pitch in the whole of Greece, but there was no sign of anyone playing today.

It wasn't long before we got to a pedestrian-only street that was blinding us with its creamy white stone paving. There was a good mix of shops, and also a lot of cafés and bars with tables outside already busy with many tourists enjoying a mid-morning drink. We were tempted but walked on to see what else might be interesting first.

Our instinct was to turn into a side street where it was quieter (and not so dazzling), and here the shops became more 'market' style with souvenirs and cheap clothing, as well as food. It was noticeable that the street was busy with local people doing their shopping, together with holidaymakers looking for bargains to take home. Unusually, we found several things to buy and some were very cheap items. They all had designer labels, and obvious fakes of course, but how could we resist a bargain?

By now it was very hot and getting more and more crowded, so it wasn't long before we found a slightly less busy corner and enjoyed an ice-cream before making our way back to the shuttle bus stop. We had not been out for very long, but we had bought some items and seen a few things to remember our visit to Corfu. We were quite sure we would be back again one day.

With legs and wallets fully exercised, we had the afternoon to relax and worship the sun once more.

This was a busy period on our cruise and after another Great British sail-away with fluttering flags and patriotic songs, 'Arcadia' sailed west overnight to the next port at the Italian island of Sicily.

It was just a short overnight trip and when we woke up for breakfast we found that 'Arcadia' was just entering the Sicilian port of Messina, and was passing a pretty little lighthouse-shaped statue, with a golden figure of the Virgin Mary at the top to welcome us. We quickly approached our berth for the day and it was time for us to go and eat. We had been to Messina before and knew that the immediate area was not too exciting, so today we had booked onto a tour going to the hillside town of Taormina.

It was a very pleasant morning out, beginning with a coach trip from the port, listening to our tour guide explaining what we would be seeing, as well as pointing out the landmarks. The sun was shining (of course) and even so early in the morning we were glad of air conditioning. When we arrived in the quite small town of Taormina we had a walking tour that gave us a brief chance to enjoy the quietness of the place, looking at the Sicilian architecture, as well as fountains and churches in the squares and the imposing cathedral. Taormina had been protected by a wall and we saw remnants of it at times, with occasional arched gateways that allowed us to see the thickness of the stonework.

There was a chance to briefly look at the Old Monastery, and its exhibition of puppets of all kinds of figures. The town is renowned for these intricate puppets that are perhaps a metre tall, and I presume they come out and get paraded around the streets on festival days.

When we got to the edge of the town we could see Mount Etna in the distance, and our guide told us we would be safe today as there is just white smoke visible.

But she didn't tell us what colour the smoke would be if we had to get worried.

Our visit now turned to the remains of a Greek open-air theatre with stone seating rising up from the stage area creating the traditional amphitheatre shape. It is still used today, but instead of using the original stage area, there was a raised area in front of some of the remaining arches and pillars. This backdrop for the stage was sensational, as the view through the arches was of the Bay of Taormina and the famous volcano.

There was time look around the theatre and climb up the seating to get the best views of the area. We found some cactus plants beside the theatre and they were so large that people have scratched graffiti into the leaves. One of the leaves was telling the world that Fiore and Luce were a bit of an item.

Before we left, our guide pointed out a quite startling sight some distance away at the top of the hill. There, virtually clinging to the hilltop, was the small village of Castelmola. At this distance we could make out the red-tiled roofs of the stone buildings and a tall white cross that must be visible miles away.

Taormina and the surrounding area really is a beautiful place, and we all left there with smiles on our faces and most people had little parcels of souvenirs to remind them.

Our visit was over, and the coach took us back to the harbour, and although we discussed having a walk around , we opted for 'Arcadia' again and lunch. The afternoon was again a chance to enjoy the sunshine before we waved goodbye to Sicily and sailed away to the west.

Tuesday 17th July was a sea-day as we crossed the Mediterranean, and a chance to really enjoy what

'Arcadia' had to offer. I really love sea-days, especially when the sun shines, and today it was shining from dawn until dusk. So a lot of time was spent horizontal on the sun loungers, with me people-watching in between periods of meditation (sleeping) as my body absorbed the heat. Deb usually read her books but even she occasionally rested her eyes as the sea gently rushed by.

By 2007 we had been regular cruisers with P&O and had achieved the highest level in their loyalty scheme. Initially this had been the P.O.S.H. Club (Port Out Starboard Home) but recently it had changed its name to the Portunas Club. Either way, we were now at Gold level and this gave us various treats such as priority boarding (virtually no queues), a welcome aboard buffet with drinks, and 10% off purchases on the ship. Today we had one of the other special moments with a Gold Portunas lunch that was hosted by an officer. This started with a champagne welcome and then serious amounts of free wine during the meal, that was to an even higher standard than the usual delicious meals. The hour-and-a-bit long meal was an extremely friendly affair chatting with the officer on our table, and the other similarly-experienced cruisers. There were not many passengers at this loyalty level, so it was quite an exclusive lunchtime experience, and we left comfortably full of food and seriously tipsy from the wine.

The evening was a formal one, and the two of us (still slightly tiddly from lunch) were dressed in our finest. The ship was an amazing sight, with all but a very small number of her passengers looking splendid in dinner jackets and long dresses. A lot of new cruisers are unhappy that they have to dress formally on four or five nights of their holiday. They argue that it is old-fashioned and no longer necessary, but the traditional ways of cruising are all part of the experience that most of us want to be maintained. The dress code is explained in the brochure, so if you don't like it then find an alternate ship. Please don't argue that it's wrong and do everything possible to rebel against it.

That night the theatre had a very special treat for us with a show called Le Cirque Arcadia, where the singers and dancers also showed off their acrobatic skills in a special performance that involved trapeze, balancing, and rope work. It was truly amazing and the audience gasped and applauded throughout the 40-minute show. We have been on 'Arcadia' on several cruises and although the theatre troupes always have acrobatic specialists, that Cirque Arcadia spectacular is no longer performed.

It had been quite a special day for us.

The next morning Captain Walters had successfully found Mallorca and was docking in the city of Palma.

Our plans were simple, with a leisurely breakfast and half an hour leaning on the rails looking at this beautiful city and watching the activities on the dock below us. With the sun smiling on us again we bounced down the gangplank a little after 9:00 am and made our way to the shuttle bus. Once we had been dropped off across the road from the Cathedral and Almudaina Palace, we took our usual stroll through the gardens including having a look at the little lake where a black swan was enjoying its breakfast.

Palma was quite familiar to us but we decided to have a change from shopping today and instead had a tour of the city on a hop-on-hop-off bus. This was the first time that we had looked beyond the Cathedral or commercial area, and allowed us a glimpse of the architectural gems of the city. We saw many beautiful sights including the fort-like Spanish Village (Poble Español), and the Belver Castle where we stopped for a while and looked at the splendid views down from this high point of the city, out across the harbour and the Bay of Palma. The bus took us around most the city and opened our eyes to many new areas, giving us some ideas for future cruises that dock here.

This was the final port of our cruise and late in the afternoon, with yet another 'Great British Sail-away' party out on deck, 'Arcadia' slipped her lines and started the final three-day trip back to Southampton.

Back at home, with the washing completed, suitcases stored in the loft, and over two weeks of post sorted out, we relaxed with a glass of wine and reflected on the 16 days aboard 'Arcadia'. It had been superb, with glorious warm weather and even the trips across Biscay had been calm and relatively warm. Our holiday had almost been perfect, but the disappointment of missing Dubrovnik was just a slight dampener.

.....never mind it made us more enthusiastic to come on the same cruise again.

+++

June/July 2009 – 'Arcadia' again

Leaving Venice on the 7th July after a superb couple of days in the Adriatic, we sailed southwards to our second Croatian port of this cruise and the city of Split. We woke to a beautiful sunny day and with the ship at anchor a little way off-shore, meaning the tenders would be taking us to the quayside. Being a new place to us, we booked a tour called 'Ancient Split and Salona' that would be taking us around the area to some Roman ruins, and the remains of the old city of Split.

It was an unusually early start (for us) and we assembled before 8:00 am in the Globe Theatre to get

119

our tickets and wait for the call to board our tender. The ride ashore was a delight and our first impressions of the city were of a clean modern harbour area, once we succeeded in looking beyond the ferries. There was little time to see much initially as our coach whisked us away to Salona some five kilometres from Split, passing a not-so-inspiring view of an oil refinery on the way.

Salona itself was a quiet archaeological site, and our visit began with a look at a very old graveyard that was being excavated for research. Apparently this was where Christian martyrs were buried once their duties with the lions had been completed. Our guide gave a very in-depth description of the graveyard and the ongoing work, which included cleaning and repairing the marble sarcophagi and cataloguing the graves and pillars that were strewn around the site.

While some of the passengers had a toilet break, there was time to look around a garden. It has a lovely variety of flowers and shrubs, with a shaded pathway under some overhanging trees set amongst various Roman relics. It was a chance to cool off here before we went back into the heat of the sun to look at an area with more remains. This time it was of the public baths, and sections of an aqueduct, and what was suggested as being an amphitheatre.

In the strong sunshine the heat was almost unbearable, and many of us took the opportunity to seek shade close to the walls rather than listen too intently to our enthusiastic guide. She eventually took pity on us and we returned to the coach and moved on to the Archaeological Museum of Split.

This was quite a spectacular building with gardens and statues outside, and a courtyard with a covered walkway crammed with Roman artefacts that the guide used, to tell the story of the city over the centuries. When we eventually went inside the museum there was free time to look around at whatever we wanted.....as well as a chance to buy souvenirs, of course.

Our last venue for the tour was in the centre of Split at the area that was the remains of the walled Diocletian's Palace. The guide was back in enthusiastic mode here as she described how it once was. Before entering the main walled area we looked at a huge statue dedicated to Bishop Grgur Ninski. It apparently gives good luck to those who rub one of its bronze toes, and Deb couldn't resist helping to keep this toe very shiny. Along with many hundreds of tourists we moved into the walled area through the Golden Gate (not much sign of gold anymore) and wandered through the alleyways to see various buildings and statues.

There was a local band playing in one of the multitude of squares that had been formed where collapsed buildings had been demolished. They were attracting a lot of people to stop and listen to traditional

121

Croatian folk songs and it was quite pleasant, but we didn't have a clue what they were singing about. Our snaking group of tourists moved on to what was once the Palace Courtyard which was packed with people speaking in languages from all over the world. Croatia attracts a huge number of holidaymakers coming to enjoy the wonderful weather, look at the archaeology, and view a country recovering from a major bloody civil war.

Below this palace there was an underground maze where people used to live and work, and there is still a market there to this day selling souvenirs to willing tourists. The main reason for our visit here was to look at the foundations of the palace above, but although interesting, the market stalls were a little more tempting.

That was the final part of our tour and when we said goodbye to our amazing guide we walked along the wonderful clean paved pedestrian area towards the dockside. There was time for an ice-cream of course, before we joined the queue for our tender ride back to 'Arcadia'.

Our visit to Split proved popular with 'Arcadia's passengers, and as well as the tour we did, others on offer included a simple accompanied walk around Split, or a look at the countryside and the Cetina River, or for the more active there was rafting on this river as well.

122

Some people went to a nearby National Park that featured waterfalls, and a longer sight-seeing trip introduced the passengers to the sights and sounds of the Split Riviera.

Some of these tours had afternoon sessions as well as morning ones, so while the ship was relatively deserted for the afternoon we both took advantage of the quiet swimming pool, and then dried ourselves in the hot sunshine. This had been a delightful day, and late in the afternoon, with everyone back on board, 'Arcadia' pulled up her anchors and set a southerly course again towards the Greek island of Corfu.

Thursday 9th July, and we arrived for our second visit to Corfu. None of the tours on offer attracted our enthusiasm so we decided to do our own thing. Unlike last time when we just looked at the shops, this time we had a plan to explore the Old Fort area. It was a hot day again and the fort is on top of a hill, so our explorations involved a significant climb over rocky areas and some steep steps.

.....we always seem to pick a hot day to climb up a hill.

Anyway, the fort was quite interesting with some spectacular views from the top. After returning to ground level we went to the shopping area again to seek out some bargains. The clothes were very good value, but like on our first visit most of the bargain items were fakes. It may be a bad decision but sometimes these fake items are just as good a quality as the real fashion clothes. Neither lasts very long but why spend three times as much? Perhaps the fashion business should realise that clothes need to be good enough to last longer than one summer if they want to stop people buying fakes.

Our visit to Corfu ended with us enjoying the sunshine on the ship and as evening approached 'Arcadia' set off again for the second Greek island on this cruise.

The next day the sky was just as clear and sunny but this time we were at anchor off the island of Zakinthos. It seemed a lovely place to have breakfast on the balcony especially as we were in no hurry to go anywhere. The morning started by eating our Danish pastries while we watched the tenders being launched below us.

The Captain made his usual welcome greeting to Zakinthos, and his deputy gave instructions for tendering, and described the arrangements on shore. We continued with our delicious breakfast knowing that only those on tours would be able to get ashore initially.

Even though this was our first visit to this island we couldn't find a tour that interested us. There was the usual panoramic coach trip and occasional walkabouts, a mini-cruise around the Blue Caves, or a simple transfer to a beach. We had already decided to go ashore when we were ready and have a walk around the town.

Just before 9:00 am the reception desk officer announced that people like us (doing our own things) could collect tickets for the tender trips, so that was our cue to pick up the usual bits and pieces and set off to explore this little Greek island.

After the gentle ride ashore we had quite a long walk around the quayside, past some slightly rusty old ferries that were no longer in use. We didn't mind the walk or the surroundings as many years of cruising, and many different ports, have made us realise that the state of the docks rarely has any similarity to the towns and cities they serve.

Once in the town of Zakinthos (same name as the island) we walked along palm tree lined streets and looked at the white buildings that are so typical of Greece. We came across Solomos Square which is apparently the hot-spot of the town in the evening, but which was rather quiet on a Friday morning. There are various statues to look at, and according to the port guide supplied by the ship, one statue is of the famous poet Dionysios Solomos, and another we liked was of Amphitrite the Greek Goddess of the sea. There was also a 15th Century church dedicated to 'Saint Nicholas on the Mole'.

We found a few shops and cafes on the streets but we were more interested in a walk rather than spending money. So we carried on along the road until we eventually arrived at a pebbled beach area, that gave us a chance for a delightful cooling paddle in the Ionian Sea.

That was enough for us, so we made our way back to the docks and a tender-ride to 'Arcadia'. It sounds a very simple and uninspiring morning out, but we were very happy with what we had done. Cruise ship holidays allow you to see many different places, and you can book tours or explore to your hearts' content. But you can also have a quieter time at a port and like us, just have a walk and then enjoy the ship on a sunny afternoon.

There is no pressure, and you can do what you want, when you want.

At the end of another perfect summer's day the anchors rattled back into 'Arcadia's hold and we set off again for two days at sea on our trip westwards across the Mediterranean and our final stop at the port of Gibraltar.

During those delightfully warm couple of days we enjoyed the chance of a swim, with periods of sun worship to doze or read a book….personally I preferred to doze. The first night was another formal one, with a ball in the Globe cabaret bar after watching a comedian in the Palladium Theatre. By now we had started to learn to dance so we spent many of our evenings practicing our crude basic waltz, or a more enterprising cha-cha that we thoroughly enjoyed.

On the second day there was a chance to visit the galley with a walkthrough past the spotlessly clean preparation areas, guarded by a few bored looking staff to stop dirty fingers touching things, which were not for touching. This was followed by the 'chocoholics' afternoon tea session where you could totally pig out on all things chocolate. Over the years we had been to a few of these and had learnt not to be too greedy in case it spoilt our evening meal. I remember when we first cruised they were held late at night and the queues were horrendous.

That evening after watching a superb show in the theatre from the Headliners, Deb entered a quiz in the Globe that was based on 'The Weakest Link' television show. I think I was involved as well but had no chance compared to Deb, who managed to beat off the competition and win us a bottle of champagne-ish. After we left the bar with Deb feeling rather pleased with herself, we sat in the quiet area outside of the Arcadian Rhodes select dining restaurant. We had a table booked in there for the next evening, so we dropped off the champagne to drink with that meal.

All in all this was quite a superb evening.

So on Monday 13th July 'Arcadia' was docked in Gibraltar by 8:00 am for a short morning-only visit. Other than the small number of new cruisers on board, most passengers had been here before, and not many people

127

had booked on the tours. The majority of us either took a short taxi ride or a bit longer walk from the quayside to the famous Main Street.

.....we walked, by the way!

A few people did go and look at the caves, and take a chance with the apes, or had a morning looking for dolphins in the bay. In the past we had done most of these touristy trips, so today it was a simple walk down the street, and a touch of window-shopping for any bargains. Even though it was just mid-morning, some of the passengers were sitting in Casemate Square, tucking into fish and chips washed down by lager before they dashed from shop to shop looking for the cheapest cigarettes and whisky.

With no interest in duty free items, we walked to the end of the shopping area and arrived at the large gate marking the end of the old walled garrison area. We might have simply turned back, but instead we carried on and stumbled on a lovely surprise. No more than a few metres past that gate and down a short set of steps is the Trafalgar Cemetery, where some very old gravestones and memorials mark the resting place of soldiers, sailors and civilians from the times of the Battle of Trafalgar. We spent nearly an hour looking at the inscriptions with stories of who lay there, and how they met their end. It is so peaceful and sheltered from the traffic noise, with just the birds talking to us for company.

After some thought-provoking time in the cemetery we walked back through the shops and found a couple of souvenirs, before strolling back to the quayside in the heat. The early morning fish and chip eaters were now struggling back along the road slightly worse for wear from the lager, carrying holdalls full of duty free delights. I am sure the officers are prepared for an increase in the weight of their ship after a stop at Gibraltar.

By 1:00 pm all the passengers were back on board and many were on the stern deck waving flags, and drinking more lager as they sung their patriotic songs while 'Arcadia' cast off and made course for home.

The major part of the holiday was over, and as we left the Mediterranean and headed north the temperature dropped and the sun became less friendly. It was time to make the most of 'Arcadia' that was now very much one of our favourite ships. We had our preferred seating spots in the split-level theatre, and favoured seats in the Globe bar. Late at night there was a cosy corner in the Intermezzo bar where we often had a nightcap.

Of course we adored the Asian food in the Orchid Room at the top of the ship, and Arcadian Rhodes thrilled us with equally-delicious food. At the stern around the Aquarius pool we spent long summer evenings with parties under the stars, or we simply relaxed in the Crow's Nest during the day or night.

The holiday had been perfect in all ways.

+++

May 2011 – 'Aurora'

Two years later, and we were on the homeward leg of another cruise to Venice. It was aboard 'Aurora' this time, and for a very good reason. In January of the following year we spent three months on 'Aurora', and we chose her for our early summer holiday to get used to her, as well as enjoying some of our favourite destinations.

After ten days on the ship we had got very used to the layout and places to enjoy during the daytime, and of course at night. The Crow's Nest was a special place in the daytime, to look around at the sea and spot other shipping, but it was also a splendid place to doze in the sunshine. The café overlooking the Atrium was a regular place to stop for a latte or mocha, while we people-watched or read the ship's daily newspaper. Our favourite eating place in the daytime was Café Bordeaux for both breakfast and lunch, but only as a treat. We ate there in the evening on a couple of occasions and enjoyed its superb menus. Evenings usually involved the Curzon Theatre for the shows and Carmen's for dancing, cabaret acts, and game shows. Champions bar was also a regular watering hole where we took part in the afternoon quizzes as well as having a late night drink before bed.

So after leaving Venice we had sailed south overnight, and on Tuesday 31st May we found ourselves at anchor in the bay just off the island of Korcula (Croatia) again. We had been here in 2007 and enjoyed its freshness as a cruise port, so had no hesitation in booking another tour. This time our trip was to the Lumbarda Vineyard for another wine-tasting session, plus a demonstration of making pasta.....and eating it of course.

This was more professional than the first little wine making business we visited, and although the pasta making was nothing to inspire us, eating it as well as several other local foodstuffs, all washed down with plenty of delicious wine, made the morning rather special.

This vineyard was attempting to do more than simply offer food and drinks to its visitors. The outside area had been landscaped with flower and vegetable patches, and there were several pens holding various animals. The goats proved a hit with most of us as they nibbled away at the bits of bush that were thrown in by the gardener. There were a couple of sculptures and a fountain in amongst the plants, and a flight of steps flanked by small pillars that just about looked Greek if you squinted.

All in all the visit was very interesting, and enjoyed by most of us.

Back at the town we revisited the market we had found on our other visit, and searched out a couple more souvenirs. We also looked at the views of the bay and went down the steps to the waterside for a paddle in the clear Adriatic waters.

The town was even busier this time and very full of younger couples. Korcula is obviously attracting younger holidaymakers from all over Europe, and it was just becoming a little noisy with modern music blasting out from the bars. We left the town to the youngsters and returned to the more sedate 'Aurora' for lunch and a quiet afternoon in the sunshine. With an early evening sail-away we had two sea days ahead of us as we sailed across the rest of the Mediterranean for our final port on the cruise at Cadiz.

During those two days and nights there were some memorable moments. A real highlight for me was when I had the chance to take part in some very amateurish dramatics. Karen, one of the entertainment officers, had taken on the daunting task of putting on a '*Who done it*' play that was to be performed in the Globe one evening. Some of entertainment team had roles, but a few passengers jumped at the chance as well.

The play was called 'Murder on the good ship 'Aurora' and was suitably overacted by everyone involved. I played the ship's Captain, dressed in the Chief Purser's cap as the Captain had no intention of anyone looking like himself. Of course virtually everyone was a suspect to the dastardly murder and the audience had to decide who was the guilty person, and the clues that led to their decision.

Well, the play was enjoyed by a fairly good-sized audience, and we had a very good time as well. I think the over indulging of Dutch Courage helped to keep us calm, but didn't improve remembering the lines, or when they were supposed to be said, or where we should be standing when we said them.

.......*all in all a very good pantomime*

Other evening entertainment included another show by the Headliners, plus a classical pianist, and a singer specialising in swing music.

The weather stayed dry and warm giving our skin an early summer treat of a bit of exposure. Captain David Pembridge had a question-and-answer session hosted by the Cruise Director, Natalie, which was both entertaining and informative about the life of a cruise ship Captain. This event happens on most cruises, and although many of the questions (and answers) are familiar, it can be a good laugh.

133

Anyone interested in a bit of exercise had the usual morning and afternoon sessions of deck quoits and shuffle-board, and the sports' net hosted the daily cricket for the men whose minds considered themselves younger than their bodies actually were.

.....yes I was one of them.

All too soon we were realising that the holiday was in its last phase, but on a cruise ship there is rarely any excuse to get bored. It doesn't matter if you are an active person or one that enjoys sitting and reading a book. 'Aurora' has a cinema with decent films each day, and sessions of bridge and quizzes every few hours are available. Oh yes, and the bars are open for most of the day to drown the sorrows of those wishing the cruise could carry on for ever.

Friday 3rd June, and overnight we had left the Mediterranean and arrived at the port of Cadiz in southern Spain just after midday. This was becoming a very regular stop for us and we had no intention of joining a tour. So we simply had a walk and looked for something to buy as a reminder of the city. It was only a short stop but many people did take to the coaches for scenic tours of this Andalusian area, or a visit to a mountain village as well as sherry tasting, and even demonstrations of Flamenco dancing. I think we have done all of these things over the years, and they are all wonderful chances to see places and experience a bit of the local culture.

Late in the afternoon there was the final sail-away deck party with the final flag-waving session, and loud singing accompanied by Sangria. Then it was time to head up the western coast of Spain towards home.

It was the last two days of a cruise that had been superb. On the last night we said goodbye to our dinner table-mates, gave our tips to the waiters and cabin steward, and left our suitcases outside the cabin door. We never drink too much on that final night knowing we have a car journey in the morning.

Monday 6th June, and by the time we woke up we were already moored at the dockside in Southampton. This is a bit of a frantic time with everyone having an early breakfast, which means longer queues at the buffet, and a search for somewhere to sit. Passengers have to be out of the cabins quickly to allow the stewards a chance to change the bedding, and clean the room for the next guests. This results in passengers sitting at any available spot with their hand luggage, and their faces rarely have a smile. Everyone has a coloured ticket to identify the approximate time they will be getting off, and regular *'bing bongs'* on the PA system produce a moment of silence as the next tickets are announced, and groups get up with *'goodbyes'* all around before they trudge off to the exits.

We had a further perk of being at the highest tier of the loyalty scheme, and that is priority disembarkation, meaning an early get-off time. While the majority of passengers were still sitting impatiently waiting to leave, we reacted to the first announcement and slipped quietly off the ship. There was the customary *'cheerio'* from the entertainment team at the gangplank as we handed back our identity cards. Then we bounced along the walkway, dragging our wheelie cases that made such an awful rumbling noise on the mottled floor material. Soon we arrived in the luggage recovery hall and now the challenge was to spot our carefully-chosen coloured cases that no-one else would have. And then discovered the vast room had hundreds of similar colour and style ones as us.

This is never a favourite moment of any cruise, but it doesn't take long. Before we knew it, we were in the car and driving the now-familiar route out of Southampton towards home.

But it wasn't long before we were planning our next cruise to Venice.

Other Books by This Author

A Cornishman Goes Cruising

The reader will first be taken through the planning and preparation stages of a supposed one-off holiday of a lifetime, before travelling with the author and his wife on a magical adventure that changed their lives.

For those of you who have already sampled a cruise holiday, this will bring back the memories of life on board a ship, with all the choices available, and the thrill of waking up to a new location each day.

Perhaps you are considering a cruise. Then this book will give you a flavour of the delights that can be expected on a fortnight's escape from normal everyday life.

Around the World without Wings

The author and his wife retired at the end of 2011 and they needed something really special to celebrate this moment.

So on a cold January evening in 2012 they left Southampton on the cruise ship MV Aurora on an adventure that would change their outlook on life, with a circumnavigation of the world lasting over three months.

Travel with them and share their thrills, laughter, and yes a few tears, as they discover so many amazing countries, cultures, and experiences on their journey around the world.

A Cornishman cruises the Western Mediterranean

The cruise ship adventures of the author and his wife (Deb) have visited many of the wonderful mainland Mediterranean ports of Spain, France and Italy, as well as numerous islands.

This volume of the Cornishman's maritime holidays, concentrates on the Western Mediterranean destinations.

Time for Tea and a Cheese Scone

Retirement at the end of 2011 brought new challenges for George and Deb, as well as the freedom from work.

The author kept a diary of the first year of retirement after over forty years of employment, and this book looks at the winter months as the couple get used to a new way of life.

Would You like Some Plums?

Following on from the first book about their retirement, this book looks at the summer months in 2013.

As the couple enjoy their release from work, they decide to move to a new home.

Along with so many different things that the couple experienced in that six months, the house move becomes a major topic of this book.

You Need a new Hip

Like many thousands of people each year the author was shocked when he was told he needed a new hip. This book shares his experiences leading up to the diagnosis and then the operation itself, plus the first year of recovery.

Hip replacements are very common but George struggled to find out more than the basic facts of what the procedure involved, and certainly very little information existed for the quite lengthy recovery period. To help others that might be waiting for a replacement, or have just had one, this book might help to clear up some of the questions and will hopefully give you confidence for the eventual outcome.

A Cornish Boy Grows Up

This book is a rework of a previous book entitled See 'e 'gen Cornwall. Although much of the material is the same, the emphasis is on the author's early years, and school life until he begins full time employment.

George Williams was born in Cornwall at a time when life was far simpler and slower than children experience today. Holidaymakers come in their thousands to Cornwall each summer, to enjoy the golden beaches, but many also become fascinated by the County's Myths and Legends. Tiny fishing villages are full of locals speaking in an accent that is both sweet and confusing to a visitor's ear, and stories are recounted of Pirates and Piskies while they eat the famous pasties or cream teas.

The author grew up with his parents and three brothers, and life was full of fun with a small group of friends, but there were

139

also some dark moments and tragedies. The lazy Cornish way of life did little to encourage George to take his education very seriously, and by the time he left school in 1968 he had only acquired a handful of qualifications to attract the interest of prospective employers.

In this book the author candidly recounts the first phase of his life, as he makes his way from infant innocence, through painful hormone changes of adolescence, to the realisation that growing up means more than playtime.

He also tries to give a flavour of Cornwall's uniqueness and beauty to those who have never sampled its delights, and attempts to share his love for the County.

Printed in Great Britain
by Amazon